EYEWITNESS
UNIVERSE

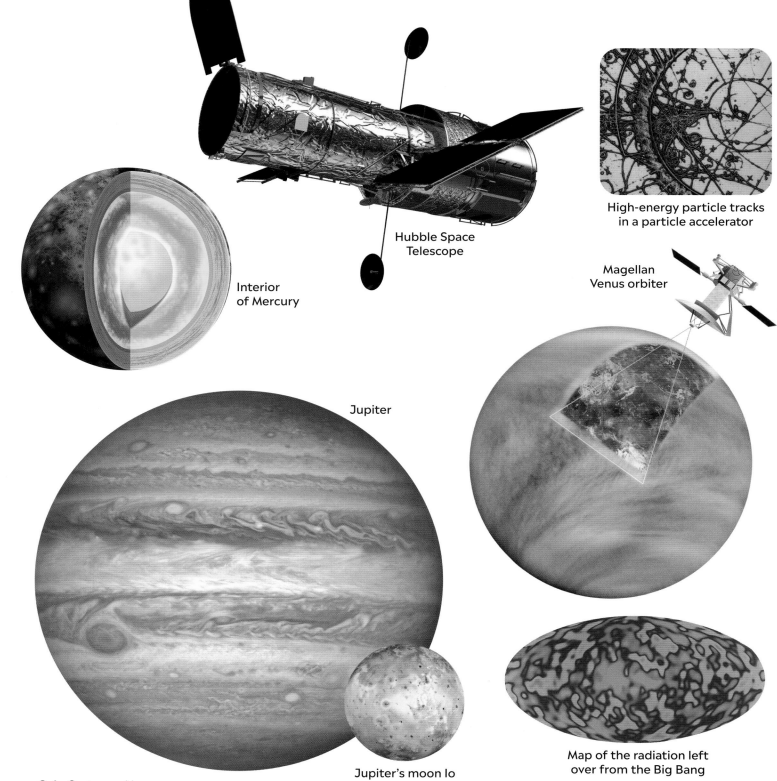

Hubble Space
Telescope

High-energy particle tracks
in a particle accelerator

Interior
of Mercury

Magellan
Venus orbiter

Jupiter

Jupiter's moon Io

Map of the radiation left
over from the Big Bang

Gale Crater on Mars

Bust of Roman
god Jupiter

Chandra X-ray
Observatory

EYEWITNESS
UNIVERSE

Written by
ROBIN KERROD

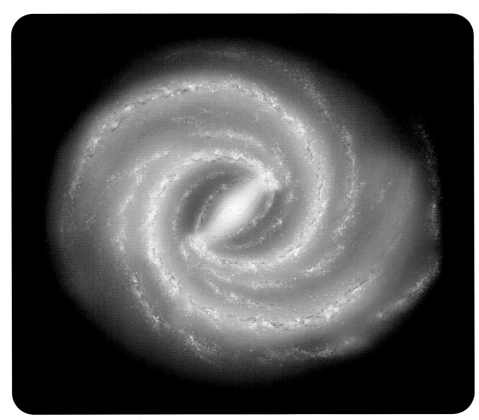

Milky Way galaxy

Mars

Core of an active galaxy

Antique spectroscope

REVISED EDITION

DK DELHI
Senior Art Editor Vikas Chauhan **Project Editor** Upamanyu Das
Project Art Editor Heena Sharma **Assistant Editor** Arpit Aggarwal
Assistant Picture Researcher Nunhoih Guite
Managing Editor Kingshuk Ghoshal **Managing Art Editor** Govind Mittal
DTP Designers Vijay Kandwal, Pawan Kumar, Deepak Mittal
Jackets Designer Vidushi Chaudhry
Senior Jackets Coordinator Priyanka Sharma Saddi

DK LONDON
Senior Editor Jenny Sich
Senior Art Editor Sheila Collins
US Senior Editor Jennette ElNaggar
US Executive Editor Lori Cates Hand
Managing Editor Francesca Baines
Managing Art Editor Philip Letsu
Production Editor Jacqueline Street-Elkayam
Production Controller Jack Matts
Senior Jackets Designer Surabhi Wadhwa-Gandhi
Jacket Design Development Manager Sophia MTT
Publisher Andrew Macintyre
Associate Publishing Director Liz Wheeler
Art Director Karen Self
Publishing Director Jonathan Metcalf

Consultant Giles Sparrow

FIRST EDITION
Project Editor Giles Sparrow
Art Editor Tim Brown
Senior Editor Kitty Blount
Senior Art Editor Martin Wilson
Managing Editor Andrew Macintyre
Managing Art Editor Jane Thomas
Category Publisher Linda Martin
Art Director Simon Webb
Production Erica Rosen
Picture Research Sean Hunter
DTP Designer Siu Yin Ho

This Eyewitness ® Guide has been conceived by
Dorling Kindersley Limited and Editions Gallimard

This American edition, 2023
First American edition, 2003
Published in the United States by DK Publishing
1745 Broadway, 20th Floor, New York, NY 10019

Copyright © 2003, 2009, 2015, 2023 Dorling Kindersley Limited
DK, a Division of Penguin Random House LLC
23 24 25 26 27 10 9 8 7 6 5 4 3 2 1
001–336551–Dec/2023

A catalog record for this book is available from the Library of Congress.
ISBN 978-0-7440-8479-5 (Paperback)
ISBN 978-0-7440-8480-1 (ALB)

DK books are available at special discounts when purchased in bulk
for sales promotions, premiums, fund-raising, or educational use.
For details, contact: DK Publishing Special Markets,
1745 Broadway, 20th Floor, New York, NY 10019
SpecialSales@dk.com

Printed and bound in China

www.dk.com

MIX
Paper | Supporting
responsible forestry
FSC™ C018179

This book was made with Forest
Stewardship Council™ certified
paper—one small step in DK's
commitment to a sustainable future.
For more information go to
www.dk.com/our-green-pledge

Sunset at Stonehenge

Earth

Very Large Array radio telescope

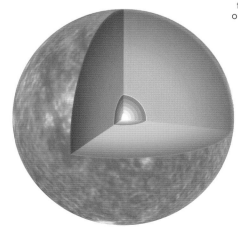

Inside a supergiant star

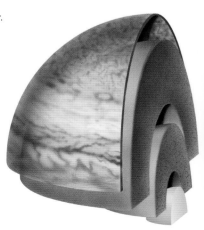

Interior of Jupiter

Contents

James Webb
Space Telescope

What is the universe?

The universe is everything that exists—today, in the past, and in the future. It is an immense space populated by innumerable galaxies of stars and filled with light and other radiation. When we look at the night sky, we are gazing at the fathomless depths of the universe and stars that are trillions of miles away. Humans have studied the universe for at least 5,000 years, through the science of astronomy.

Floating in space
Earth might seem tiny in the vast scale of the universe, but it's still precious as the only place we know of where life has evolved. The first people to see the entirety of Earth from space were the Apollo astronauts who traveled to the moon in the 1960s and '70s.

Early astronomy
The ancient Britons knew about the movements of the sun, moon, and stars. In around 2600 BCE, they completed Stonehenge—circles of standing stones that marked the positions of the sun and moon during the year.

Babylonian astrological tablet

Astrology
Ancient Babylonians thought that things that happened in space could affect humans on Earth. Even today, many people follow this belief, called astrology.

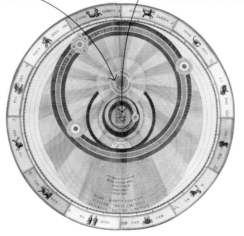

The sun orbits Earth.

Earth at the center of the Ptolemaic Universe

Ptolemy's universe
In around 150 CE, the Alexandrian Greek astronomer Ptolemy wrongly theorized that Earth was at the center of the universe and everything else moved around it.

World in motion

In 1543, Polish astronomer Nicolaus Copernicus theorized a sun-centered universe where Earth and the other planets travel around the sun in circular orbits. Later, German Johannes Kepler (right) discovered that the planets travel around the sun, not in circles, but in ellipses.

Johannes Kepler
(1571–1630)

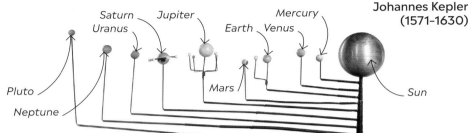

Saturn | Jupiter | Mercury
Uranus | | Earth | Venus
Pluto | | Mars | Sun
Neptune

Planetary pathways

Kepler's laws of planetary motion explained that the planets move around the sun. In 1687, English mathematician Isaac Newton found that it was a force called gravity that kept the planets in the sun's orbit.

Mechanical model (orrery)
of the solar system

Stars and galaxies

By the late 1700s, astronomers began to figure out what our galaxy was like. By plotting the distribution of stars, German British astronomer William Herschel showed that our galaxy is lens-shaped (we now know that it is a spiral with a bulge in the center). In 1923, US astronomer Edwin Hubble discovered the first galaxy outside our own— the Andromeda galaxy (right).

A vision from the past

When we look into space, we are looking back in time because the light from distant objects has taken so long to reach us. Space telescopes, such as the Hubble Space Telescope (see pp.16–17), enable us to peer even deeper into space. This Hubble image (left) is called the Ultra Deep Field— it shows around 10,000 galaxies, including some of the most distant galaxies known.

How do we **fit in?**

Not long ago, people thought our planet was the center of the universe. In fact, it is an insignificant rock in a small galaxy, in one tiny corner of space. No one knows how big the universe is, but the most distant galaxies we can see are an unimaginable distance of 13.8 billion light-years from Earth.

Medieval world map

Pancake planet?

In ancient times, many people thought the world was a flat disc floating in space, with the known continents surrounded by a circular outer ocean.

Scale of the universe

This sequence of images shows how we fit into the bigger picture, going from life at the human scale to the immensity of intergalactic space. We use light-years to measure distances in space. One light-year is the distance that light can travel in a year—5.9 trillion miles (9.5 trillion km).

From space, Earth looks blue due to the vast expanses of surface water. White clouds surround the planet.

In the solar system, Earth is the third planet out from the sun. It would take more than eight minutes to travel to the sun at the speed of light.

Runners in a marathon cross a crowded bridge.

This satellite view shows the city from hundreds of miles above Earth.

Our view of the universe

We look out at the universe from inside a layer of stars that forms the disc of our galaxy. Along the plane of this disc, the galaxy extends for tens of thousands of light-years. In the night sky, we see this dense band as the Milky Way. By combining different satellite images of the sky, we can see what the universe looks like from inside our galaxy.

👁 EYEWITNESS

Margaret Geller

US astronomer Margaret Geller is a professor at the Harvard Center for Astrophysics, and a pioneer of techniques for mapping the distribution of galaxies. Her maps have helped reveal the structure of the universe, showing that galaxies are grouped together in thin sheetlike structures around voids (empty spaces).

Traveling at the speed of light, it would take millions of years to reach most galaxies in the nearby universe, and billions to reach those even further away.

The Oort Cloud of cometlike bodies forms a boundary around the solar system. At the speed of light, it would take a year or more to reach the outer edge of the Oort Cloud.

Our galaxy—the Milky Way—contains billions of stars. It would take four years to reach the next nearest star to the sun, Proxima Centauri.

These dark regions represent areas where dust from the Milky Way obscures our view of the universe.

Venus

Earth

Jupiter

Saturn

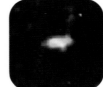
Uranus

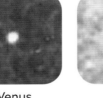
Neptune

Probing photos

Space probes have taught us much about the planets in our solar system. On a 12-year mission, the Voyager probes visited Jupiter, Saturn, Uranus, and Neptune. In 1990, a photo taken by Voyager 1 as it departed our solar system made the planets look like tiny specks lost in the vastness of space.

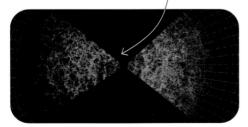

The local universe

In this map of our local region of the universe, each dot of color represents a galaxy. It shows that galaxies cluster together, forming threadlike filaments with voids in between.

How the universe works

The universe is made up of islands of matter in an ocean of empty space. Energy travels through the universe as light and other radiation. Four fundamental forces dictate what matter is like and how it behaves. The strongest of the four binds particles together, while the weakest, gravity, holds the universe together.

Elements and atoms

Empedocles (above) believed matter was made up of fire, air, water, and earth. His fellow Greek philosopher, Democritus, thought instead that matter was made of tiny bits he called atoms. Hundreds of years later, English chemist John Dalton confirmed Democritus's theory.

Radio waves (wavelengths 1 mm or more)

Infrared (700 nm to 1 mm)

Peak

Trough

Trough

Wavelength

A family of waves

The radiation that carries energy through the universe takes the form of electromagnetic waves. There are many kinds of radiation, differing in wavelength—the distance between one peak or trough of the wave and the next. Visible light is radiation that our eyes see as colors from violet to red, with wavelengths between 390 and 700 nanometers (one nanometer is a billionth of a meter). Invisible wavelengths are shorter than violet light and longer than red.

INSIDE ATOMS

An atom is the basic unit of matter. Atoms themselves are made up of even smaller, "subatomic" particles. The three main particles are protons and neutrons, found inside an atom's nucleus, and electrons, which circle the nucleus.

Water molecule made from one oxygen and two hydrogen atoms.

Water droplet

Inside an atom, electrons orbit a tiny nucleus.

Protons have a positive electric charge.

Electrons have a negative electric charge.

Neutrons have no charge.

Protons and neutrons are made up of even tinier particles called quarks.

Probing the atom

Physicists use incredibly powerful machines called particle accelerators, or "atom smashers," to investigate the structure of atoms. These machines use beams of subatomic particles to smash up atoms, revealing their inner structure.

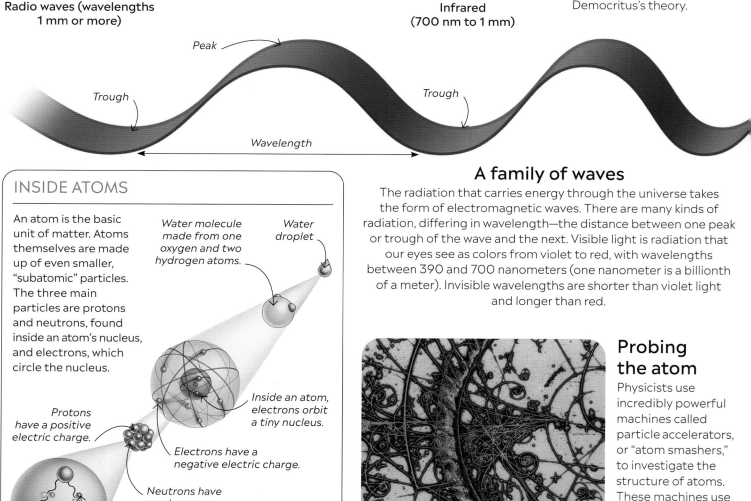

Particle tracks as seen at a European nuclear research center in Geneva

Grades of gravity

English scientist Isaac Newton established the basic law of gravity: that every body attracts every other body because of its mass. The bigger a body, the greater its gravitational attraction. Saturn's enormous gravity keeps rings of particles circling its equator and at least 83 moons in orbit around it.

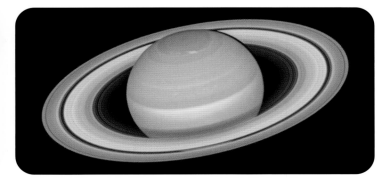

Saturn and its rings photographed by the Hubble Space Telescope

Iron filings reveal invisible lines of magnetic field.

Similar poles of magnets repel each other.

Magnetism

Magnetism is the force that makes magnets attract iron filings. When suspended, a magnet will align itself north-south, in the direction of our planet's magnetic field. Earth's magnetism extends far out into space, creating a bubble-like region called the magnetosphere.

Ultraviolet (10 nm to 390 nm)

X-rays (0.001 nm to 10 nm)

Gamma rays (up to 0.001 nm)

Visible light (390 nm to 700 nm)

NASA's infrared Spitzer Space Telescope

Spitzer's view of the Milky Way

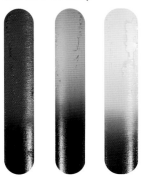

Temperature and color

Heating an iron poker causes it to glow and give off shorter and shorter wavelengths of light—first red, then orange and yellow. If you heat it enough, it would glow white and eventually blue. The same is true of stars—the hottest blue-white ones have temperatures ten times greater than the coolest red ones.

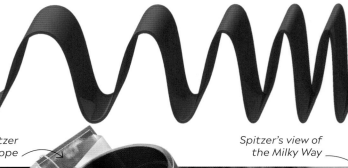

The hidden universe

We see the universe as it appears in visible light. But objects in the universe may also give out radiation at invisible wavelengths. Some types of invisible radiation, such as infrared, can be accurately studied from Earth's orbit using space telescopes.

In the **beginning**

We have a good idea of what the universe is like today and what makes it tick. But where did it come from? How has it evolved? What will happen to it in the future? The branch of astronomy that studies these questions is called cosmology. Most cosmologists agree that an explosive event called the Big Bang created the universe around 13.8 billion years ago. They are not so certain about how the universe might end (see p.15).

Part of a multiverse?

Some astronomers say that our universe could be just one of a vast number that are continuously being created from the same Big Bang, forming an infinite "multiverse." These other universes could be very different from our own.

Big Bang creates the universe, which is infinitely small, infinitely hot, and full of energy.

Energy from the Big Bang creates particles of matter and antimatter, which annihilate one another.

As the universe cools, combinations of particles become stable.

Evolving universe

Three minutes after the Big Bang, the temperature of the universe fell from countless trillions of degrees to a billion degrees. This cooling allowed the conversion of energy into the subatomic particles that would seed the first galaxies about 380,000 years later.

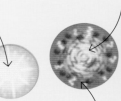

A fraction of a second into its life, the universe expands to an enormous size.

Universe expanding from Big Bang

As the universe cools down, quarks become the dominant type of matter.

Quarks collide to form protons and neutrons.

Electrons and positrons are formed.

Clear universe

Until the universe was about 380,000 years old, it was full of particles and opaque. Then electrons combined with atomic nuclei to form the first atoms. The particles then cleared, and the universe became transparent.

Matter too dense for light to travel freely

Temperature drops and electrons are soaked up into atoms.

Most electrons and positrons annihilate each other.

Matter condenses to form galaxies and clusters.

Georges Lemaître

Belgian priest Georges Lemaître (1894–1966) was a leading astronomer and cosmologist. After predicting that the universe is expanding, he traced its origins back to a hot, superdense "primeval atom" that exploded. His suggestions gave rise to the Big Bang theory.

Temperature is steadily dropping.

Light waves bounce off particles before traveling far, just as in a fog.

Photons now travel freely in largely empty space.

Decoupling photons are the earliest we can detect.

Echoes of the Big Bang

Penzias and Wilson with their radio horn antenna

In 1965, physicists Arno Penzias and Robert Wilson picked up weak radio signals coming from the sky with a cosmic background temperature of around –454°F (–270°C). This is the temperature scientists calculated would follow the Big Bang.

Red areas are warmer and emptier.

Blue areas are colder and denser.

Ripples in the cosmos

The COBE (Cosmic Background Explorer) satellite made the first accurate map of the cosmic microwave background radiation (CMBR)—left over from the Big Bang. It shows the "lumpiness" of the early universe.

Studying the past

Launched in 2009, the European Space Agency's Planck satellite measured CMBR in greater detail, mapping temperature differences to the nearest millionth of a degree. This allowed astronomers to study what the universe was like at just 300,000 years old.

A small number of electrons survive.

Protons and neutrons form atomic nuclei.

Electrons still unattached

Electrons combine with nuclei to form atoms.

The universe as it is today, full of galaxies, stars, and planets, and still expanding

The universe is still opaque. Radiation prevents matter from clumping together.

The universe becomes transparent as matter starts to condense.

Fate of the universe

Ever since the universe was created in the Big Bang, it has been expanding. But will this expansion carry on forever, or might it eventually slow down or even reverse? The answer—and the fate of the universe—depends on the amount of visible and unseen matter in the universe, and the strength of a mysterious force called dark energy.

The expanding universe

Using the Hooker telescope (above) to study the expanding universe, American astronomer Edwin Hubble (see p.59) discovered that the more distant a galaxy is, the faster it is moving away from Earth. This results in longer (redder) wavelengths from that galaxy.

Spectrum of light from a laboratory source (standard)

Spectrum of light from galaxy moving away from us (redshifted)

Redshift

Astronomers use a method called spectroscopy to study light from stars. In one form of spectroscopy, the spectrum of light from stars contains gaps or lines where certain elements in the star or space absorb some wavelengths. For stars or galaxies moving away from us, these gaps appear shifted toward the "red end" of the spectrum. This is called redshift. It means an increase in the wavelength of light reaching us from those stars or galaxies. This provides evidence that space is expanding.

👁 EYEWITNESS

Vera Rubin
US astronomer Vera Rubin (1928–2016) devoted her career to measuring the light of distant galaxies. In the 1970s, she discovered that the outer visible stars in galaxies orbit the galactic center much faster than scientists expected—this meant they were being affected by something around each galaxy—important evidence for the existence of dark matter.

Galaxies were closer together in the early universe.

Present-day universe

Big Bang—origin of the universe's expansion

Universe, many billions of years ago, when the first galaxies formed

Universal expansion

You can imagine the expanding universe by thinking of it as a balloon with the galaxies scattered on the surface. As the balloon expands, the galaxies are pushed farther apart. The expansion of the universe was set in motion by the Big Bang, but it is also driven by a mysterious force called dark energy, which is currently speeding up the expansion.

The light from this galaxy has been distorted by the gravity of a nearby galaxy as a result of its extremely high mass, caused by the presence of dark matter.

Trails in a particle detector

Missing mass

Effects such as gravitational lensing (the bending of light rays by gravity, as seen above) reveal that many galaxies and galaxy clusters have much higher mass than can be accounted for by their visible matter. The unseen "dark matter" outweighs visible matter by about six to one.

Big Chill
In this scenario, the universe eventually runs out of fuel to form new stars, ending in a "Big Chill."

Dark particles

Dark matter is not made up of faint stars or planets—instead scientists think it is made of "WIMPs" (Weakly Interacting Massive Particles). These are particles that are both invisible and transparent to light, but have a small amount of mass. Astronomers and physicists use particle detector experiments to search for them.

Time

Expansion
Dark energy causes the universe to expand forever.

Big Crunch
In this scenario, gravity pulls the universe back together into a "Big Crunch."

Big Rip
In this scenario, dark energy keeps getting stronger and the universe continues to expand, eventually ending in a "Big Rip."

Possible fates

The fate of the universe depends on the balance between gravity (created by visible and dark matter) pulling inward, and the universe expanding outward. Astronomers used to think that gravity might eventually beat expansion and pull the universe back to a "Big Crunch," where all its matter is pulled together into an infinitely small point. The discovery of dark energy now suggests that the universe may keep expanding forever. However, nobody knows for sure.

Big Bang
This is the starting point of the universe.

Exploring space

Astronomers have spent more than five millennia gazing at the stars, comets, planets, and moons in the heavens above us. A giant leap in astronomy came when Italian scientist Galileo Galilei (see p.33) first turned a telescope on the skies in 1609. Since then, larger telescopes have revealed a universe more extensive than anyone could have imagined. Other telescopes study the invisible radiations stars and galaxies give out.

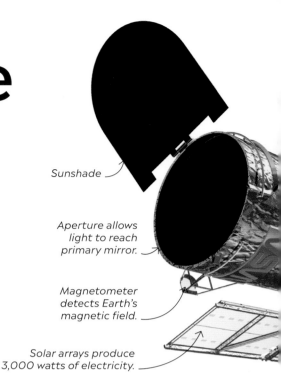

Sunshade

Aperture allows light to reach primary mirror.

Magnetometer detects Earth's magnetic field.

Solar arrays produce 3,000 watts of electricity.

LIGHT REFLECTOR

Most astronomical telescopes use a large, curved primary mirror to gather and focus light, reflecting it back along the telescope tube onto a secondary plane (flat) mirror. This mirror in turn reflects the light into an eyepiece mounted near the front of the tube.

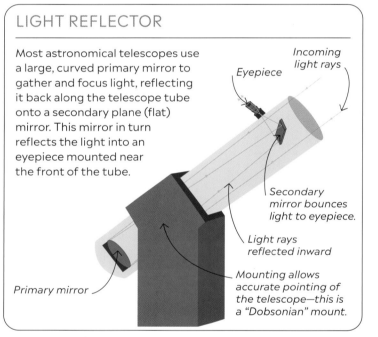

Incoming light rays

Eyepiece

Secondary mirror bounces light to eyepiece.

Light rays reflected inward

Mounting allows accurate pointing of the telescope—this is a "Dobsonian" mount.

Primary mirror

Hubble Space Telescope

The Hubble Space Telescope (HST) is a reflector with a 7.9 ft (2.4 m) diameter mirror. It circles Earth every 90 minutes in an orbit about 380 miles (610 km) high. Above Earth's atmosphere, Hubble views the universe with perfect clarity, not only at visible wavelengths but in the ultraviolet and infrared as well.

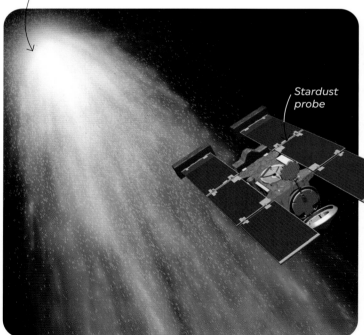

Comet Wild 2

Stardust probe

Twin Kecks

The two Keck telescopes in Hawai'i have light-gathering mirrors measuring 33 ft (10 m) across, made up of 36 separate segments. Each segment is individually supported and computer-controlled so together they always form a perfect mirror shape.

Probing space

Stardust is a space probe that flew by Comet Wild 2 in 2004 and captured comet dust, which it returned to Earth just over two years later. Probes have been exploring space since 1959.

Insulating foil prevents expansion and contraction during temperature changes.

Radio astronomy

Radio astronomers must use huge dishes to collect radio signals from space. Many observatories use sets of dishes in unison to form effective collecting areas miles across. The Very Large Array radio telescope, near Socorro in New Mexico uses 27 dishes in various configurations.

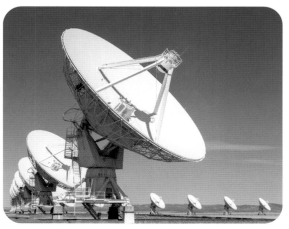

Telescopes of the Very Large Array

Position of primary mirror

Instrument segment houses cameras and spectrometers.

High-gain antenna

Access panels allow individual instruments to be replaced.

Integral

High-energy telescopes

Some telescopes, such as Integral, can detect high-energy radiation from the most violent regions of the universe—around quasars, supernovas, and black holes.

Infrared giant

Launched in 2021, the James Webb Space Telescope (JWST) is an infrared telescope with a gold-plated 21 ft (6.5 m) mirror, designed to study faint nearby objects as well as the most distant galaxies in the universe. The telescope's huge sun shield protects its mirror and instruments from heat from the sun and Earth.

Artist's impression of the JWST

A secondary mirror reflects signals picked up by the main mirror onto the central camera.

Mirror segments help focus faint infrared radiation from distant stars.

Camera module

Layered heat shields reflect heat away from the mirror.

The JWST's control systems are located here.

17

Our solar system

Ancient astronomers believed Earth was the center of the universe. Today, we know the sun is at the center of our corner of the universe, and Earth and the other planets circle that body. They are part of the sun's family, or solar system. Eight planets, including Earth, are the most important members of the solar system, along with five known dwarf planets, more than 230 moons, and billions of asteroids and comets.

Moons
All the planets except Mercury and Venus have satellites, or moons, circling them. This is Saturn's moon, Mimas.

Planets
A planet is a world massive enough to pull itself into a roughly spherical shape that orbits the sun. Earth is the third planet from the sun.

Mercury

Mars

Neptune takes 165 years to orbit the sun.

Jupiter takes 11.9 years to orbit the sun.

All eight planets follow orbits close to the plane of the sun's equator, which is called the "plane of the ecliptic."

Uranus takes 84 years to orbit the sun.

Jupiter

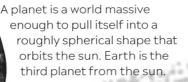

Uranus

Saturn takes 29.5 years to orbit the sun.

Map of the solar system
The planets orbit the sun at different distances, from about 36 million miles (58 million km) to about 2.8 billion miles (4.5 billion km). The planets don't move in perfect circles but in elliptical (oval) orbits.

Gas and dust collapse into a disc.

Central regions heat up.

Sun blows away surrounding gas cloud.

Planets form as increasingly large particles come together.

How it all began

Around 4.6 billion years ago, there was nothing in our corner of space but a huge billowing cloud of gas and dust. Then, after millions of years, the cloud began to collapse and spin under gravity. Over time, a thick disc of matter formed, which became progressively denser and hotter, and evolved into our sun and then the planets.

Asteroid Ida

Asteroids

Asteroids are lumps of rocks and sometimes metal left over from the formation of the solar system. They are found mainly in a region known as the Asteroid Belt, although some asteroids stray close to Earth. In 1995, the probe Galileo photographed the 35-mile (55 km) long asteroid Ida on its way to Jupiter.

Comets

Comets are icy bodies that form a vast sphere called the Oort Cloud, which surrounds the planetary part of the solar system, far beyond the Kuiper Belt.

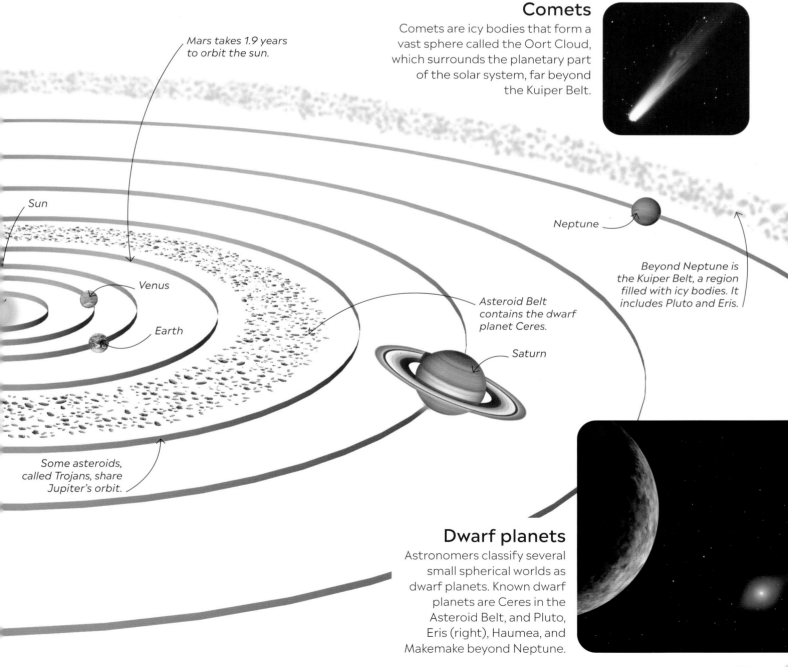

Mars takes 1.9 years to orbit the sun.

Sun

Venus

Earth

Some asteroids, called Trojans, share Jupiter's orbit.

Asteroid Belt contains the dwarf planet Ceres.

Saturn

Neptune

Beyond Neptune is the Kuiper Belt, a region filled with icy bodies. It includes Pluto and Eris.

Dwarf planets

Astronomers classify several small spherical worlds as dwarf planets. Known dwarf planets are Ceres in the Asteroid Belt, and Pluto, Eris (right), Haumea, and Makemake beyond Neptune.

Our
local star

The star we call the sun dominates our corner of space. With a diameter of 870,000 miles (1,400,000 km), it is more than 100 times wider than Earth. The sun is a great ball of incandescent gases, and lies 93 million miles (150 million km) away from Earth. It provides the light and warmth needed for life to flourish on our planet.

Prominences are fountains of hot gas above the surface.

Sun worship
In ancient Greek mythology, the sun god Helios carried the sun across the heavens every day in a flying chariot.

The solar cycle
The sun's magnetism gives rise to sunspots, prominences (above), and huge outbursts called flares. Magnetism and activity vary over an 11-year solar or sunspot cycle.

Sunspots can persist for weeks and grow to the size of planets.

The visible surface is called the photosphere. The temperature here is about 9,900°F (5,500°C).

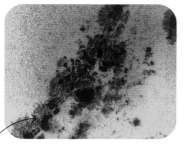

Sunspots
Sunspots are dark patches on the sun, about 2,700°F (1,500°C) cooler than the surrounding surface. They include "pores" 600 miles (1,000 km) across.

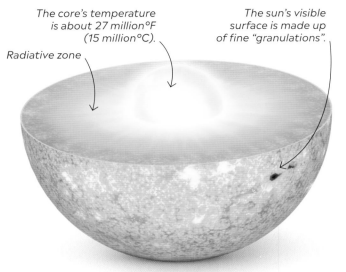

The core's temperature is about 27 million°F (15 million°C).

The sun's visible surface is made up of fine "granulations".

Radiative zone

Inside the sun

The sun is hottest and most dense at its center, or core. There, fusion reactions combine hydrogen atoms into helium, producing the energy that keeps the sun shining. Energy takes over a million years to transfer from the sun's core to the surface.

SOLAR WIND

The sun's corona gives off a steady stream of tiny, charged particles called the solar wind. This blows at a speed of hundreds of miles per second and, like weather on Earth, the intensity of the solar wind can vary. The solar wind hits Earth's magnetic field, or magnetosphere, which deflects most of it into space (see p.29).

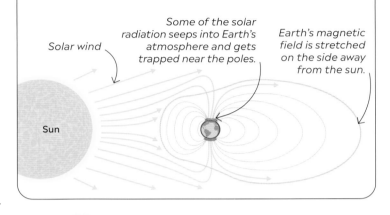

Solar wind

Some of the solar radiation seeps into Earth's atmosphere and gets trapped near the poles.

Earth's magnetic field is stretched on the side away from the sun.

Sun

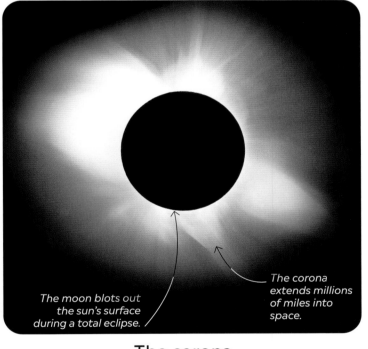

The moon blots out the sun's surface during a total eclipse.

The corona extends millions of miles into space.

The corona

An atmosphere of gases surrounds the sun. Temperatures in the white outer atmosphere, or corona (meaning "crown"), can hit 5.4 million°F (3 million°C).

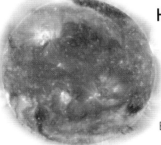

High-energy sun

The sun radiates not only light and heat but also ultraviolet rays (seen in this ultraviolet image) and X-rays. These are dangerous forms of radiation that are mostly blocked by Earth's atmosphere.

Parker Solar Probe

The sun's intense heat makes it difficult to observe up close, but in 2018 NASA launched a heavily shielded robot spacecraft designed to fly through the sun's corona, recording conditions and analyzing the sun's atmosphere.

The sun was born with **enough fuel** in its core to shine steadily for **10 billion years**.

Earth's moon

The moon is Earth's closest companion in space and its only natural satellite. On average, it lies 239,000 miles (384,000 km) away. It has no light of its own but shines by reflecting sunlight. As the moon circles Earth, it appears to change shape, from a slim crescent to full circle, and back again every 29.5 days. With a diameter of 2,160 miles (3,476 km), the moon is a rocky world like Earth, but has no atmosphere, water, or life.

Bright crater surrounded by rays

Moon's near side

Lunar gravity

Earth spins around its axis once a day.

Oceans bulge out

Moon's gravity pulls at oceans.

The moon's gravity is only one-sixth of Earth's, so it cannot retain any gases to make an atmosphere. The lack of atmosphere means the temperature on its surface varies from 230°F (110°C) to –290°F (–180°C). Weak though it is, the moon's gravity still affects Earth. It tugs at the oceans to create tides.

Low tide

High tide

Neil Armstrong
US astronaut Neil Armstrong (1930–2012) flew naval aircraft before joining NASA in 1962. After his first flight to space in 1966, he served as commander of Apollo 11 in 1969—the first crewed mission—becoming the first human to set foot on the moon.

Craters formed when meteorites crashed into the moon.

The changing face
The changing phases of the moon happen as the sun lights up different amounts of the side that faces Earth. During the new moon phase, we can't see it because the sun is lighting up only the far side. As the moon moves around in its orbit, more and more of its face gets lit up.

New moon

Crescent

First quarter

Waxing gibbous

Full moon

Waning gibbous

Last quarter

Decrescent

The face of the moon

The moon always presents the same face toward Earth. This happens because it spins once on its axis in exactly the same time as it circles once around Earth—27.3 days. This motion is called captured rotation. The dark regions we see on the moon's face are vast dusty plains, although early astronomers thought they might be seas.

The far side

No one had seen the moon's far side until the first blurred images of it were taken in 1959. It is more rugged than the nearside and has no large "seas."

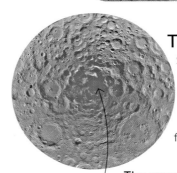

The hidden poles

Space probes have shown that some polar craters could contain deposits of ice. If proven, this ice could provide water for future human explorers.

Aitken Basin is the largest crater on the moon.

The moon's south polar region

Dark maria (seas) are plains of solidified lava.

Walking on the moon

In 1969, Apollo 11 astronauts Neil Armstrong and Buzz Aldrin planted the first human footprints on the moon. They were the first of 12 US astronauts to explore the surface, set up scientific stations, and collect samples of soil and rock.

Lunar highlands

Earthrise

The Apollo astronauts took stunning photographs of the moon, including dramatic shots of Earth rising over the moon's horizon. These showed the contrast between our colorful, living world and its drab, dead satellite.

The moon's dark seas were formed as molten lava erupted and filled deep craters more than 3 billion years ago.

Comparing the planets

Going out from the sun, the solar system's eight planets are Mercury, Venus, Earth, Mars, Jupiter, Saturn, Uranus, and Neptune. The four small inner planets are made up mainly of rock, and the four giant outer ones are made up mainly of gas. Each planet orbits the sun and also spins on its own axis.

The planets to scale

The planets vary widely in size. Jupiter contains more matter than all the other planets put together. It could swallow more than 1,300 planets the size of Earth. Our home planet could itself swallow 18 planets the size of Mercury, which is smaller than the largest moons of both Jupiter and Saturn.

JUPITER
Diameter: 88,846 miles (142,984 km)
Distance from sun:
484 million miles (778 million km)
Rotation period: 9.93 hours
Time to orbit sun: 11.9 years
Known moons: 95

MERCURY
Diameter: 3,032 miles (4,880 km)
Distance from sun: 36 million miles (58 million km)
Rotation period: 59 days
Time to orbit sun: 88 days
Known moons: 0

EARTH
Diameter: 7,918 miles (12,742 km)
Distance from sun: 93 million miles (150 million km)
Rotation period: 23.93 hours
Time to orbit sun: 365.25 days
Known moons: 1

VENUS
Diameter: 7,521 miles (12,104 km)
Distance from sun: 67 million miles (108 million km)
Rotation period: 243 days
Time to orbit sun: 225 days
Known moons: 0

MARS
Diameter: 4,212 miles (6,780 km)
Distance from sun: 142 million miles (228 million km)
Rotation period: 24.6 hours
Time to orbit sun: 687 days
Known moons: 2

Most gas giants have turbulent atmospheres.

Orbits to scale

The diagram below shows the distances of the planets from the sun (to scale). The inner planets are close together, while the outer planets are far apart.

Mercury
Earth
Venus Mars
Jupiter
Saturn

The sun is
500 times more massive
than all the planets put together.

In the ecliptic

The planets circle the sun close to a flat plane called the "plane of the ecliptic." In Earth's skies, the ecliptic is the path the sun appears to take through the heavens during a year.

The five naked-eye planets aligned along the ecliptic

An extensive system of rings surrounds Saturn's equator, spanning a distance of more than 250,000 miles (400,000 km) out from the edge of the planet. All four giant planets have ring systems.

SATURN
Diameter: 72,367 miles (116,464 km)
Distance from sun: 890 million miles (1,433 million km)
Rotation period: 10.66 hours
Time to orbit sun: 29.5 years
Known moons: 83

As shown by the tilt of Saturn's rings, planets do not orbit the sun bolt upright—most are tilted over to some extent.

URANUS
Diameter: 31,518 miles (50,724 km)
Distance from sun: 1.8 billion miles (2.9 billion km)
Rotation period: 17.24 hours
Time to orbit sun: 84 years
Known moons: 27

NEPTUNE
Diameter: 30,599 miles (49,244 km)
Distance from sun: 2.78 billion miles (4.49 billion km)
Rotation period: 16.11 hours
Time to orbit sun: 165 years
Known moons: 14

Rocky planets

The four inner planets, from Mercury to Mars, have a rocky structure. They have a thin, hard outer crust, which overlays another thicker layer, called the mantle. In the center is a core of metal, mainly iron.

Crust   Mantle   Core

Atmosphere

Structure of Mars

Gas and ice giants

The four planets from Jupiter to Neptune have outer atmospheres made mostly of hydrogen and helium. Lower down, Jupiter and Saturn transform to oceans of liquid gas, while Uranus and Neptune have mantles of slushy ice.

Liquid hydrogen

Outer atmosphere

Metallic hydrogen

Structure of Jupiter

Possible solid core

Inner worlds

Two rocky planets, Mercury and Venus, orbit closer to the sun than Earth. Both planets are hotter than Earth—surface temperatures on Mercury can rise as high as 840°F (450°C), and on Venus, up to 86°F (30°C) higher. But the two planets are quite different. Mercury has a very thin atmosphere, whereas Venus's dense atmosphere stops us from seeing its surface.

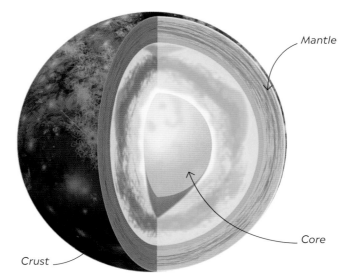

Mantle

Core

Crust

Inside Mercury

Mercury is a small planet, with a diameter of 3,032 miles (4,880 km). Like Earth, Mercury is made up of a hard outer crust, a rocky mantle, and an iron core.

SPEEDY ORBIT

Mercury orbits the sun in just 88 days, but rotates only once every 59 days. This means Mercury rotates three times every two orbits (as shown below).

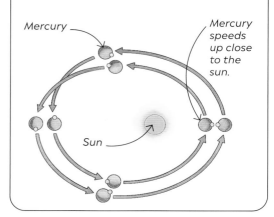

Mercury

Mercury speeds up close to the sun.

Sun

The cratered surface

Mercury was bombarded with meteorites billions of years ago, resulting in the cratered landscape we see today. Caloris Basin is one such crater, 800 miles (1,300 km) across.

Mercury

Sun's surface

Transits

Mercury and Venus circle the sun inside Earth's orbit and sometimes pass in front of the sun as seen from Earth. We call these rare crossings "transits."

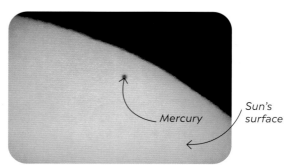

Cook's tour

In 1768, Britain's Royal Society sent James Cook on the first European scientific expedition to the Pacific Ocean. In Tahiti, Cook recorded the transit of Venus, which could be used to measure the distance from Earth to the sun. Cook later sailed his ship *Endeavour* to New Zealand and Australia.

Clouds of sulfuric acid

Earth's deadly twin

Venus and Earth are almost identical in size but are very different worlds. Venus is a hostile planet, with high temperatures, a crushing atmosphere of carbon dioxide, and clouds made up of droplets of sulfuric acid. No human could survive there for even a minute.

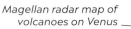
Magellan radar map of volcanoes on Venus

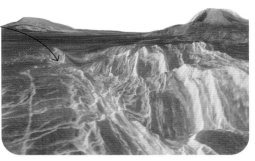

Solar panels

Magellan probe

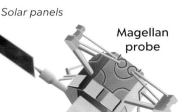

Radar antenna

Surface of Venus below the clouds

Volcanic world
Venus's surface has been shaped by volcanoes, some of which may still be active today. Waves of lava flows can be seen where they have erupted. Geological activity has also created circular coronae and spidery networks called arachnoids.

Through the clouds
We can't see the surface of Venus, but mapping by space probes such as Magellan have revealed it to be a mostly low-lying planet with a few highland regions. The largest are two outcrops, Ishtar Terra and Aphrodite Terra.

Goddess of love
Venus was the Roman goddess of love, and most of the planet's features are named after women, such as the crater Cleopatra, a plain called Guinevere, and a deep valley called Diana.

Venus de Milo in the Louvre, Paris

Venus's surface
Early last century, people had no idea what Venus was like. Some hoped it would contain life. The first close-up pictures of the surface by the Russian Venera probes in the 1970s and '80s revealed the planet to be baked, barren, and devoid of any life whatsoever.

19th-century artist's impression of Venus's surface

1982 Venera photograph of Venus's surface

Home
planet

With a diameter of 7,926 miles (12,756 km), Earth is Venus's near twin in size, but the similarity ends there. At 93 million miles (149.6 million km) from the sun, Earth is a haven for life, unlike lifeless Venus. It is a rocky planet, but its surface is made up of plates instead of being solid.

Earth's oceans are more than 2.5 miles (4 km) deep on average.

Plate tectonics
The study of Earth's shifting crust is called plate tectonics. Often, colliding plates destroy rocks and create volcanoes.

Inside Earth
Earth has a layered structure like an onion. It has an outer layer, or crust, of thin, hard rock, averaging about 25 miles (40 km) on the continents and about 6 miles (10 km) under the oceans. The crust overlays a heavier rocky mantle with a soft top. Deeper down lies a huge iron core. The outer core is liquid, while the inner core is solid.

Earth seen from orbit

Oceans and atmosphere
Oceans cover more than 70 percent of Earth's surface. The evaporation of ocean water into the atmosphere plays a crucial role in the planet's climate and dictates weather patterns around the world.

Antarctica

Death Valley, California

Climate extremes

Antarctica recorded the lowest ever temperature of –138.5°F (–94.7°C), while temperatures often hit 122°F (50°C) in Death Valley, California.

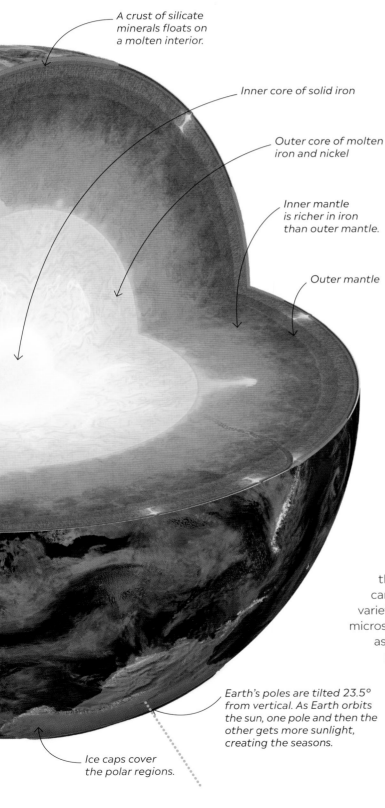

A crust of silicate minerals floats on a molten interior.

Inner core of solid iron

Outer core of molten iron and nickel

Inner mantle is richer in iron than outer mantle.

Outer mantle

Ice caps cover the polar regions.

Earth's poles are tilted 23.5° from vertical. As Earth orbits the sun, one pole and then the other gets more sunlight, creating the seasons.

Aurora photographed from space

The magnetic shield

Earth's magnetism creates the magnetosphere—a cocoon around the Earth that shields it against the sun's deadly radiation. Charged particles from the sun—the solar wind (see p.21)—are mostly trapped by Earth's magnetosphere. Some particles pass through it and collide with the atmosphere, creating beautiful light displays that we call the auroras.

Life in abundance

With comfortable temperatures, liquid water, and oxygen in the atmosphere, Earth can support an amazing variety of life. This includes microscopic organisms such as bacteria, to towering redwood trees and all sorts of animals.

Life thriving on and around a coral reef

Exploring the surface

The surface of Mars has been more extensively explored than that of any planet other than Earth. Spacecraft have photographed its landscape from orbit and probes that have landed on it have taken close-up pictures of its surface. This picture of the planet's Gale Crater was taken by the Curiosity rover in 2015. The latest rovers to explore the planet are Perseverance and Zhurong, which arrived in 2021.

Mars, the
Red Planet

Mars is the planet most similar to Earth, but it is still a very different world. It is about half the size of Earth, and its day is only about half an hour longer than our own. Mars also has seasons, an atmosphere, and ice caps at the poles. But the planet's thin atmosphere, freezing temperatures, and lack of a protective magnetic field make its surface hostile to life.

The Valles Marineris canyon system is 4 miles (6 km) deep in places.

Low-lying plains cover the northern half of Mars.

The planet's southern hemisphere is dominated by cratered highlands like those on the moon.

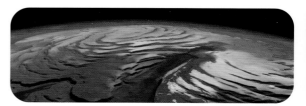

A watery past

Mars is covered in floodplains and dry river beds, which show that it once had plentiful surface water and perhaps even oceans. Satellite studies of the Martian soil reveal that much of this water is now a permanently frozen layer of ice on the surface and underground, as seen in this photograph of the Martian north pole.

An aerial view

After landing on Mars, the Perseverance rover released a small, four-bladed aircraft called Ingenuity to test powered, controlled flight on Mars, and whether similar aircraft could be used in future missions. Using its high-speed rotors, Ingenuity flew through the thin Martian atmosphere, reaching heights of 59 ft (18 m) and covering a distance of more than 6.8 miles (11 km) in over 50 flights.

On top of the world

Olympus Mons is the largest of four volcanoes near Mars's equator. It is 15 miles (24 km) high—nearly three times higher than Mount Everest—and has a crater 56 miles (90 km) wide. It last erupted about 25 million years ago.

Moons of Mars

Mars has two tiny moons, Phobos and Deimos. Phobos measures about 16 miles (26 km) across and Deimos just 10 miles (16 km) across.

Phobos

Deimos

Martian weather

Strong Martian winds reaching 186 mph (300 km/h) often whip up surface dust to create dust devils (left) and massive dust storms.

Living on Mars

Could humans live on Mars? Space agencies and private space exploration companies plan to send crewed missions to Mars in the coming decades. This artist's impression shows a possible base for astronauts to stay and work in during their time on Mars.

King of the planets

More massive than all the other planets put together, Jupiter is the largest member of the solar system after the sun. As a gas giant planet, Jupiter has an atmosphere of hydrogen and helium above an ocean of liquid hydrogen. Its upper atmosphere is marked by dark belts and pale zones, which are clouds that have been stretched out by the planet's rapid rotation. Jupiter spins around once in less than 10 hours.

Wind speeds in Jupiter's atmosphere can reach 400 mph (650 km/h).

Ruler of the gods

Jupiter is an appropriate name for the king of the planets—its name has been inspired by Jupiter who was the king of the gods in Roman mythology.

Heat from nuclear fuel powers the spacecraft.

Antenna sends data back to Earth and receives instructions.

Galileo

The space probe Galileo reached Jupiter in 1995 after a six-year journey through space. Galileo orbited Jupiter for nearly eight years, studying the giant planet and its moons. In 2016, a follow-up probe called Juno arrived to continue its work.

Earth to same scale

Great Red Spot

Jupiter's Great Red Spot is a super hurricane, with winds swirling around at high speeds. The Spot towers 5 miles (8 km) above the surrounding cloud as the swirling currents rise. It changes in size but averages about 25,000 miles (40,000 km) across.

Target Jupiter

In 1994, fragments of Comet Shoemaker-Levy 9 smashed into Jupiter after the planet had disrupted the comet's orbit. The impacts created huge fireballs and stirred up chemicals from the lower atmosphere.

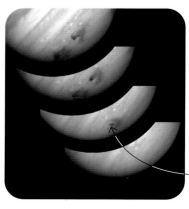

The plume (bottom) and the developing scar were made by the impact of a comet fragment.

Sulfur-covered surface

Io

The colorful moon Io is covered with sulfur flows from its many volcanoes. Volcanic eruptions also shoot plumes of gas 150 miles (250 km) above Io's surface.

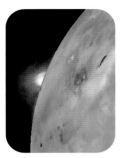

Volcanic eruption on Io

Europa's surface reflects light well.

Europa

Europa has a network of grooves and ridges that crisscross its icy crust. Beneath this frozen surface lies a deep ocean of liquid water warmed by undersea volcanoes.

Cracks in Europa's surface ice

Light areas seem to show where ice has welled up from inside Ganymede.

Ganymede

Ganymede, with a diameter of 3,273 miles (5,268 km), is the biggest moon in the solar system. Ganymede has an old icy surface, with dark areas and paler grooved regions. Recent craters show up white, where fresh ice has been exposed.

Dark regions of older surface

Callisto

Callisto orbits further out than Ganymede and looks quite different, being almost completely covered with craters. Its crust preserves scars from billions of years of impacts.

Icy surface has darkened over long periods.

Younger craters expose bright, fresh ice.

Galileo's moons

Italian scientist Galileo Galilei was among the first to observe the heavens through a telescope (above) in 1609. He saw mountains on the moon, sunspots, and Venus's phases. He also saw Jupiter's four biggest moons (left), now called "Galilean" moons.

Ringed Saturn

Saturn is one of the most distinct planets because of the glorious system of shining rings that circles its equator. It is the sixth planet from the sun and the second largest after Jupiter, measuring 74,900 miles (120,536 km) across. Saturn is composed mainly of hydrogen and helium around a rocky core, like Jupiter, but is even less dense. It is, in fact, so light that it would float on water.

The ring cycle

Saturn's axis is tilted at an angle of nearly 27 degrees, so we see its rings at various angles during its 29.5-year trip around the sun.

Shadow cast by Saturn across rings

F ring

B ring

Ring world

Saturn's ring system is dominated by three bright rings—the A, B, and C rings. The broadest and brightest ring is the B ring, while the faintest is the C ring. The B ring is separated from the A ring by the Cassini Division, and there is a smaller gap, called the Encke Division, near the outer edge of the A ring. Several broad, faint rings extend much farther from the planet.

Inside the rings

Saturn's rings are made up of thousands of narrow ringlets formed from chunks of dirty water ice whizzing round in orbit at high speed.

Giovanni Cassini
Italian-born astronomer Giovanni Cassini (1625–1712) established the Paris Observatory in France in 1671. From there, he discovered four of Saturn's moons, as well as a thin gap (later named the Cassini Division) running all the way around the planet's rings. This was the first proof they could not be a single solid object.

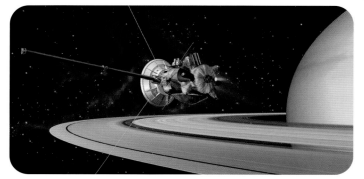

Exploring Saturn

Between 2004 and 2017, the robot space probe Cassini explored Saturn and its moons. Among Cassini's many discoveries were complex structures in Saturn's rings, lakes of liquid methane on Titan, and watery seas on Enceladus, as well as a huge electrical storm raging beneath the gas giant planet's clouds.

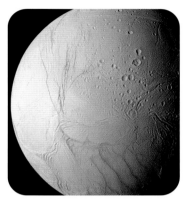

Saturn's rapid rotation makes it bulge out at the equator.

Stormy bands

The bands in Saturn's atmosphere are streams of gases coursing around the planet at high speeds and in opposite directions, creating storms.

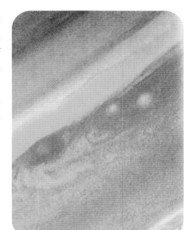

Brilliant Enceladus

Saturn's sixth-largest moon, Enceladus, has the brightest surface of any object in the solar system. It is covered in fresh snow, formed where water from seas beneath the surface erupts in plumes near the moon's south pole.

B ring

Cassini Division

D ring

C ring

Encke Division

Inner A ring

Outer A ring

Infrared photos help us peer through Titan's clouds.

Planet-size moon

With a diameter of 3,200 miles (5,150 km), Titan is bigger than Mercury, and the second-largest moon in the solar system after Ganymede. Cold conditions this far from the sun allow it to hold on to a thick, hazy atmosphere.

Sunlight glints off a hydrocarbon lake on Titan

Through the clouds

In 2005, the Huygens lander launched by Cassini parachuted through Titan's clouds to land on its surface. Images taken by Huygens revealed a surface shaped by rainfall and flowing liquid—not water but oily chemicals called hydrocarbons at temperatures of around −290°F (−179°C).

Outer worlds

Few people imagined there might be planets beyond Saturn before 1781, when German British astronomer William Herschel discovered one. Later named Uranus, this planet orbited the sun at twice the distance of Saturn, so the discovery doubled the size of the known solar system. Planet hunters discovered another "ice giant" planet, Neptune, in 1846, and a much smaller world called Pluto in 1930. Pluto is just one of many small bodies that orbit at the edge of the solar system.

Planet probe

Most of our knowledge about the planets Uranus and Neptune comes from the Voyager 2 probe. Launched in 1977, it spent 12 years visiting the four giant planets. By the time it reached Neptune, Voyager 2 had journeyed for 4.4 billion miles (7 billion km).

Cameras

Scientific instruments

Dish antenna

Magnetometer boom

Uranus

The third-largest planet, Uranus has a diameter of about 31,770 miles (51,118 km) and a deep atmosphere, with warm oceans beneath.

Methane colors the atmosphere blue-green.

The planet's axis is tipped over at an extreme angle of 98 degrees. This means that some regions experience a day and a night lasting up to 21 years during each 84-year orbit around the sun.

Temperature at cloud tops can get as low as –345°F (–210°C).

Hydrogen and helium are the main gases in the atmosphere.

Miranda

Moons of Uranus

Uranus has at least 27 moons. Made up of rock and ice, they are all different. Ariel has deep cracks running across its surface. Miranda has all kinds of different surface features jumbled together.

Cracked crust

Ariel

Neptune

This planet lies 1 billion miles (1.6 billion km) beyond Uranus. It is slightly smaller than its neighbor, with a diameter of 30,780 miles (49,532 km), and has a fainter ring system. The atmosphere is flecked with bright clouds and sometimes with dark storm regions. It is bluer than Uranus because it contains more methane. Wind speeds on Neptune are the highest in the solar system, reaching up to 1,243 mph (2,000 km/h).

Dark spots are lower in the atmosphere than bright, high-speed "scooters."

Cloud temperature is –345°F (–210°C).

Finding Neptune

In 1846, French mathematician Urbain Le Verrier predicted a new planet whose gravity, he said, was affecting Uranus. German astronomer Johann Galle soon found the new world exactly where Le Verrier said it would be.

Triton's geysers

Triton is the largest of Neptune's 14 moons, 1,680 miles (2,710 km) across. It is a deep-frozen world, covered with frozen nitrogen and methane, but is warm enough inside to power active geysers spurting a mix of nitrogen gas and dust.

Uranus has a total of 13 rings around its equator.

Ring particles average about 3 ft (1 m) across.

Pluto's moon, Charon, is 751 miles (1,208 km) across.

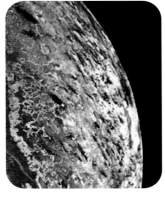

Icy outcasts

With a diameter of 1,473 miles (2,370 km), Pluto is smaller than Earth's moon. When the New Horizons probe flew past this distant icy world in 2015, it revealed a landscape that shows clear signs of activity such as freshly erupted ice and mountain building.

Pluto lies, on average, 3,670 million miles (5,900 million km) from the sun.

The outer ring is the brightest.

Asteroids and **meteors**

The solar system has many members besides planets, dwarf planets, and moons. Rocky asteroids orbit close to the sun while smaller icy bodies called comets lurk mostly at the edge of the solar system. When comets fall toward the sun and become active (see p.40), they leave behind trails of particles. Along with rocky chunks that break off asteroids, these are known as meteoroids. When meteoroids enter Earth's atmosphere, most burn up as meteors, also called shooting stars.

Asteroid Ida

The Asteroid Belt

About 400,000 individual asteroids have been identified, but there are billions of smaller ones. Most circle the sun between the orbits of Mars and Jupiter, in a broad band called the Asteroid Belt.

Different sizes

Asteroid Ida, which is 35 miles (55 km) long, is one of the many asteroids in the Asteroid Belt. The largest asteroid in this belt, Ceres, is only 580 miles (930 km) across, making it less than one-third the size of the moon. The next largest, Pallas and Vesta, are about half the size of Ceres, but most asteroids are much smaller—Gaspra, for example, is only about 11 miles (18 km) long. Gaspra, like many asteroids, is mostly made up of silicate rocks.

The celestial police

In 1800, Hungarian astronomer Baron Franz von Zach organized some "Celestial Police" astronomers to look for a planet in the "gap" in the solar system between Mars and Jupiter. However, they were beaten to it by Italian astronomer Giuseppe Piazzi, who was the first to spot an asteroid —Ceres—on January 1, 1801.

Giuseppe Piazzi
(1746-1826)

Asteroid mining

The metallic asteroids are rich in iron, as well as nickel and other metals that are comparatively rare on Earth. Metals in asteroids exist in pure form, not in ores as on Earth, and this makes them much easier to extract. In the future, humans may mine the asteroids.

Meteorite containing iron deposits

Eros

*NEAR-
Shoemaker
spacecraft*

Near Eros

In 2001, the NEAR-
Shoemaker probe made the
first landing on an asteroid, called Eros,
after studying it from orbit for a year.

Meteor shower

The streaks of light
we see in the night sky
are meteors. They are
produced by meteoroid
particles little bigger
than sand grains. As
they move through
the atmosphere. the
particles cause
the gas atoms in the
atmosphere to glow.

**The 1833 Leonid meteor
storm over Niagara Falls**

*Ida's deeply
gouged surface
probably formed
as it broke up
from a larger
asteroid millions
of years ago.*

*NASA's Nomad
robot locates
meteorites
in Antarctica.*

*Meteorites stand out
in a rockless landscape.*

Looking for meteorites

Meteoroids that survive passage through the
atmosphere are called meteorites. Astronomers
value them as a rare bit of space material they can
study on Earth—they usually search for them in
barren landscapes that have no other rocks.

*Gaspra has fewer craters
than Ida—it probably also
formed in a breakup.*

**Asteroid
Gaspra**

**Manicouagan
crater, Quebec**

*Crater rim now
forms a lake that is
used as a reservoir.*

*Crater floor may hide
huge nickel deposits.*

Ceres

The largest asteroid, Ceres, is
also considered the largest of all
dwarf planets. Bright spots on its
heavily cratered landscape are
caused by salty brine seeping up
from the mantle below through
icy volcanoes.

**Ceres photographed by
the Dawn space probe**

Impact craters

From time to time, really big meteorites smash into
Earth's surface and gouge out large craters. Around
200 million years ago, a meteorite created this
crater in Canada, which is now partially filled with water.

Icy wanderers

Huge chunks of icy debris lurk in the outer reaches of the solar system. Each of these is the city-size nucleus of a comet—a dirty snowball that remains invisible unless it travels in toward the sun and is heated up. It then develops a large head and tails. At their brightest, comets can rival the brightest planets in our night sky and can develop tails that stretch for millions of miles.

Heart of a comet

NASA's Deep Impact (EPOXI) spacecraft captured this image of comet Hartley 2's nucleus (right) in 2010. The nucleus, which measures about 1.6 miles (1 km) in diameter, is made up of water ice with methanol, carbon dioxide, and ethane.

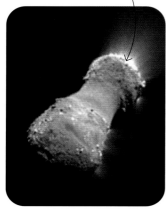

Jets of carbon dioxide gas burst from the surface.

Straight gas tail streams away, driven by solar wind (particles from the sun).

Gas tail glows as solar wind strikes gas from comet.

The nucleus is too small to be seen inside comet's glowing coma.

Fragile snowballs

Like snowballs, comets are not firmly held together and often break up. In 1992, a comet passed close to Jupiter and was ripped apart by the giant planet's gravity. The fragmented comet, called Shoemaker-Levy 9, collided with Jupiter two years later (see p.32).

Halley's Comet

English astronomer Edmond Halley was the first to discover that some comets are regular visitors to Earth. He deduced a comet he saw in 1682 was the same one that had appeared in 1531 and 1607. He predicted that it would return in 1758.

Comet Bernardinelli-Bernstein has the largest nucleus of any known comet, around 80 miles (130 km) wide.

Comet of the century

While most short-period comets are fairly faint, long-period ones from the edge of the solar system are unpredictable. Occasionally, they can outshine even the brightest stars to become a "Great Comet." Comet Hale-Bopp of 1997 (above) didn't quite achieve that, but it remains the brightest comet of recent decades, with two well developed tails streaming away from its bright head, or coma.

Dust tail is comet dust reflecting sunlight.

Dust tail curves, affected by the sun's gravity.

Orbit of Neptune

Orbit of Saturn

Orbit of Uranus

Tail leads comet as it recedes from the sun.

Short-period comet from Kuiper Belt orbits in a few decades.

Tail follows comet as it approaches the sun.

Long-period comet from Oort Cloud orbits in centuries or more.

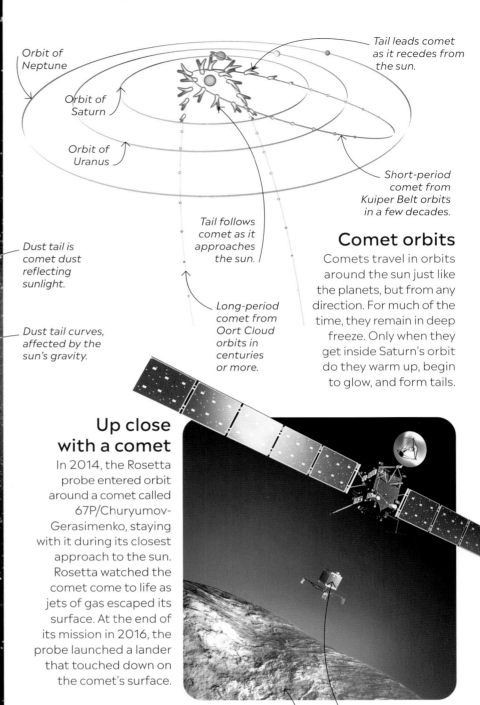

Comet orbits

Comets travel in orbits around the sun just like the planets, but from any direction. For much of the time, they remain in deep freeze. Only when they get inside Saturn's orbit do they warm up, begin to glow, and form tails.

Up close with a comet

In 2014, the Rosetta probe entered orbit around a comet called 67P/Churyumov-Gerasimenko, staying with it during its closest approach to the sun. Rosetta watched the comet come to life as jets of gas escaped its surface. At the end of its mission in 2016, the probe launched a lander that touched down on the comet's surface.

Surface of the comet 67P/Churyumov-Gerasimenko

The Philae lander deployed by the Rosetta probe

Oort Cloud

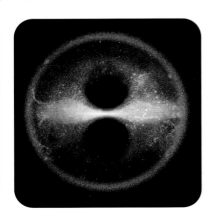

Most comets originate in the Oort Cloud, a vast sphere that surrounds the planetary part of the solar system and contains trillions of comets. It extends out to 9.4 trillion miles (15 trillion km) from the sun.

👁 **EYEWITNESS**

Dr. Bonnie Buratti

NASA astronomer Bonnie Buratti specializes in studying the icy surfaces of bodies in the outer solar system. She played an important role in the Deep Space 1 mission to fly past comet Borrelly in 2001 and later provided her expertise on the Rosetta mission as a project scientist.

Distant suns

On a clear night, you could probably count as many as 2,500 stars in the sky. They always appear as tiny pinpricks of light, but they are actually huge, bright bodies similar to the sun. However, even the closest star to the sun—Proxima Centauri—lies more than four light-years away from Earth.

Binary stars

About half of the stars in our galaxy formed in pairs, called binaries, or larger groups, called multiples, that still orbit around each other. Often the stars are so close together or so far away from Earth that they appear as a single star.

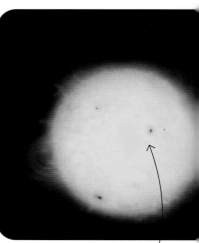

The stars of Algol are very close together.

A universe of stars

In the Milky Way, stars appear crammed together in the millions. Each star has a different brightness, color, size, and mass. There are around 200 billion stars in our galaxy alone.

HOW FAR AWAY?

The distance to the nearest stars can be measured by the parallax method. Astronomers use the method by viewing a nearby star first from one side of Earth's orbit, then from the other. They measure the amount a star appears to move against more distant stars, to calculate its distance.

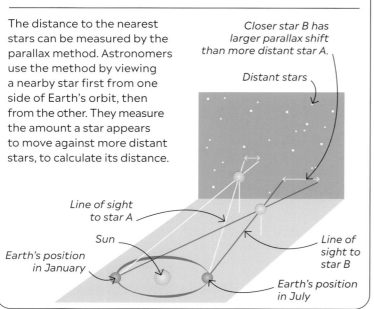

Closer star B has larger parallax shift than more distant star A.

Distant stars

Line of sight to star A

Sun

Earth's position in January

Line of sight to star B

Earth's position in July

Star brightness

The stars in constellations differ in brightness, as seen here in Orion. Astronomers use the word magnitude to describe the brightness of a star. Apparent magnitude is how bright a star looks from Earth. Rigel and Betelgeuse have similar apparent magnitudes—they look equally bright from Earth. Rigel is actually brighter, but it is farther away from Earth.

Betelgeuse

Rigel

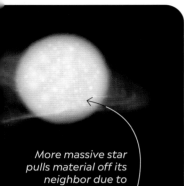

More massive star pulls material off its neighbor due to its closeness and gravitational force.

Artist's impression of Algol star system

STAR CONSTELLATIONS

Some of the bright stars form patterns in the sky called constellations. Ancient astronomers named them after figures from their myths and legends. The constellation stars look the same distance from Earth, but that is only because they lie in the same direction.

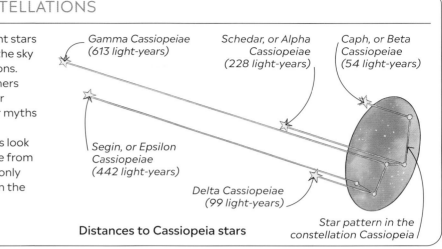

Gamma Cassiopeiae (613 light-years)

Schedar, or Alpha Cassiopeiae (228 light-years)

Caph, or Beta Cassiopeiae (54 light-years)

Segin, or Epsilon Cassiopeiae (442 light-years)

Delta Cassiopeiae (99 light-years)

Star pattern in the constellation Cassiopeia

Distances to Cassiopeia stars

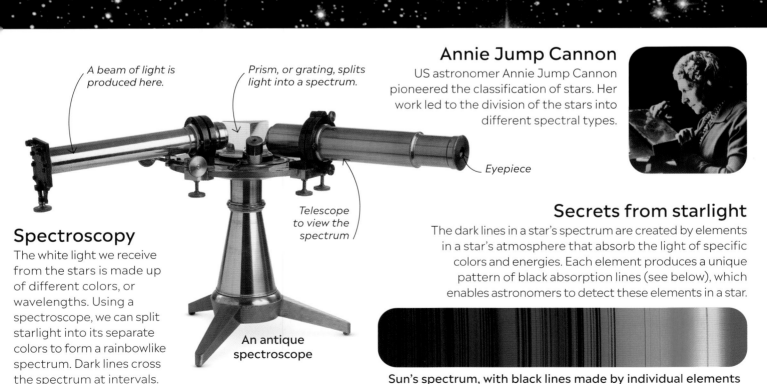

A beam of light is produced here.

Prism, or grating, splits light into a spectrum.

Eyepiece

Telescope to view the spectrum

An antique spectroscope

Spectroscopy

The white light we receive from the stars is made up of different colors, or wavelengths. Using a spectroscope, we can split starlight into its separate colors to form a rainbowlike spectrum. Dark lines cross the spectrum at intervals.

Annie Jump Cannon

US astronomer Annie Jump Cannon pioneered the classification of stars. Her work led to the division of the stars into different spectral types.

Secrets from starlight

The dark lines in a star's spectrum are created by elements in a star's atmosphere that absorb the light of specific colors and energies. Each element produces a unique pattern of black absorption lines (see below), which enables astronomers to detect these elements in a star.

Sun's spectrum, with black lines made by individual elements

The variety of **stars**

Studying the spectra of stars tells us all about their composition, color, temperature, speed of travel, and spin. Other techniques allow astronomers to measure the distance to stars and their mass. Stars vary enormously. There are dwarfs with only a hundredth the diameter of the sun and supergiants thousands of times the sun's size.

Colors and sizes

A range of typical stars is shown across this page. The most luminous (brightest) are at the top, the hottest on the left, and the coolest on the right. Stars get bigger as luminosity increases, and the most luminous are either bright blue or orange-red. A star's color depends on the amount of energy it emits.

First dwarf

Stars similar to the sun end their lives as white dwarfs, which gradually fade away. Sirius B (left) was the first white dwarf discovered.

Supergiants are the biggest stars of all, hundreds of millions of miles across.

Blue stars are tens of times bigger than the sun.

White dwarfs are tiny, hot stars only about the size of Earth.

Line of main sequence

THE HERTZSPRUNG-RUSSELL DIAGRAM

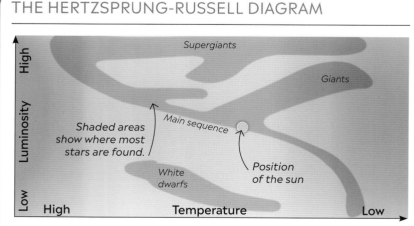

Shaded areas show where most stars are found.

Main sequence

Position of the sun

White dwarfs

Supergiants

Giants

From around 1910, Danish astronomer Ejnar Hertzsprung and US astronomer Henry Norris Russell independently developed a diagram that compares the luminosity of stars with their color and temperature. The majority of stars lie along a diagonal strip from bright blue to faint red called the main sequence—our sun is a main-sequence star.

Yellow sun

The sun is an average star of a type known as a yellow dwarf. Its color reflects its surface temperature, which is around 9,900°F (5,500°C).

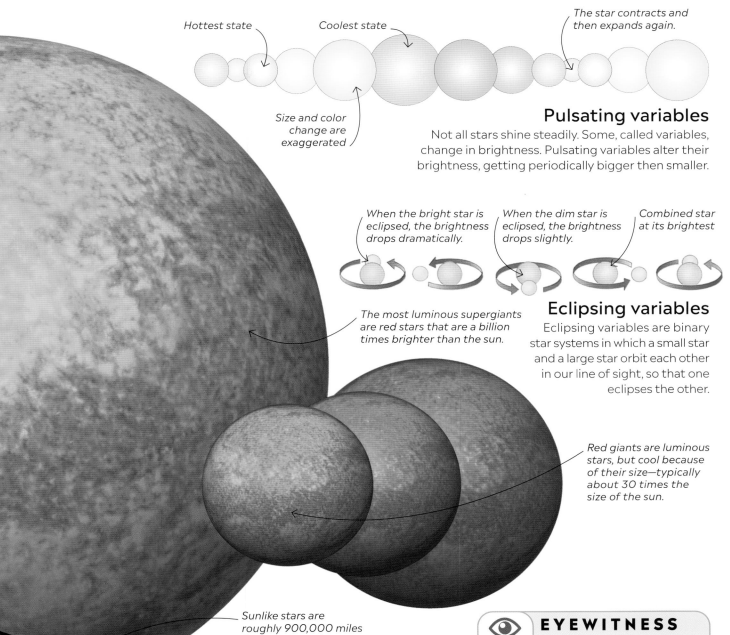

Hottest state

Coolest state

The star contracts and then expands again.

Pulsating variables

Not all stars shine steadily. Some, called variables, change in brightness. Pulsating variables alter their brightness, getting periodically bigger then smaller.

Size and color change are exaggerated

When the bright star is eclipsed, the brightness drops dramatically.

When the dim star is eclipsed, the brightness drops slightly.

Combined star at its brightest

Eclipsing variables

Eclipsing variables are binary star systems in which a small star and a large star orbit each other in our line of sight, so that one eclipses the other.

The most luminous supergiants are red stars that are a billion times brighter than the sun.

Red giants are luminous stars, but cool because of their size—typically about 30 times the size of the sun.

Sunlike stars are roughly 900,000 miles (1,500,000 km) across.

Red dwarfs are about a tenth of the size of the sun, with a surface temperature of about 5,500°F (3,000°C).

Red dwarfs are a million times less luminous than the sun.

The Winking Demon

In the constellation Perseus, a variable star named Algol marks the eye of Medusa, the snake-haired Gorgon killed by the ancient Greek hero Perseus. Algol, or "the Winking Demon," dips in brightness every 2.9 days.

Clusters and **nebulae**

Using telescopes, we can see fuzzy patches in space. Some patches are groupings of stars, known as clusters. Open clusters are loose collections of a few hundred stars and globular clusters are dense groupings of thousands of stars. Other fuzzy patches are regions of glowing gas called nebulae, which are found in the space between stars.

EYEWITNESS

Charles Messier
French astronomer Charles Messier (1730–1817) was an expert comet hunter who found himself frustrated by other fuzzy objects in the sky. To help his search, he compiled a catalog of noncomet objects such as star clusters and nebulae. Published in 1774, Messier's catalog is still used by astronomers to this day.

Globular cluster NGC 1466 is packed with ancient orange stars.

Globes of stars
Globular clusters are made up of hundreds of thousands of stars packed together in a ball. They contain mostly ancient stars, around ten billion years old.

Open clusters
The best-known of all open clusters is the Pleiades, in the constellation Taurus. It is also called the Seven Sisters. In total, the Pleiades contains more than 100 stars, all of them hot, blue, and young—probably less than 80 million years old. Most open clusters contain stars that are similar to each other.

Alcyone

Pleione

Atlas

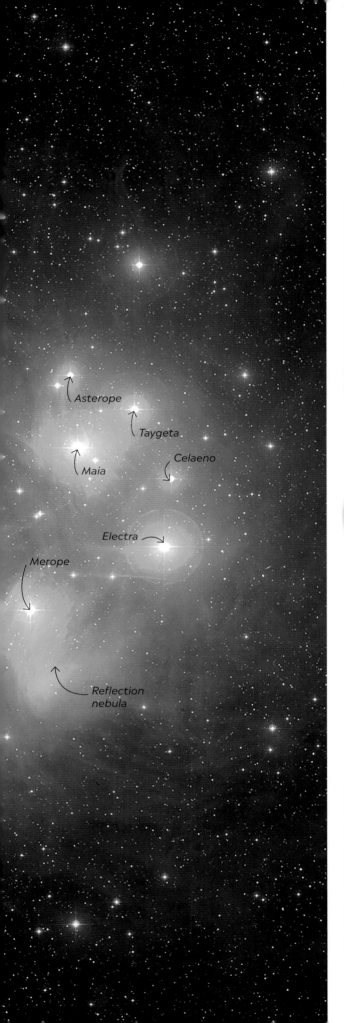

Asterope

Taygeta

Maia

Celaeno

Electra

Merope

Reflection nebula

Between the stars

The space between the stars is not empty. It contains gas and dust known as the interstellar medium. The interstellar medium is visible as bright and dark nebulae, and accounts for a tenth of the mass of our galaxy.

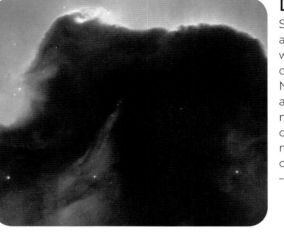

Dark nebulae

Some clouds of gas and dust are lit up, while others remain dark. The Horsehead Nebula (left) is a well-known dark nebula in the Orion constellation. Dark nebulae are generally cold, around –436°F (–260°C).

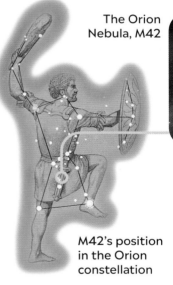

The Orion Nebula, M42

M42's position in the Orion constellation

Bright nebulae

Many interstellar clouds are lit up by stars. Some of them reflect starlight. Others are bright because the radiation from nearby stars causes gases in the cloud to glow. These are called emission nebulae. A famous example is the Orion Nebula, which is part of the Orion constellation.

Stellar remnants

Stars are born from nebulae, and give rise to nebulae when they die. Sunlike stars first swell up to become red giants, then shrink into tiny white dwarfs. As they do so, they give off layers of gas, known as planetary nebulae.

Planetary nebula Mz3 is sometimes called the Ant Nebula.

Star birth

Stars are born in giant gas clouds that occupy interstellar space. Within these clouds, made up mainly of hydrogen, gravity pulls the gas molecules together to make dense clumps, and even denser cores. As gravity makes a core collapse in on itself, it becomes hotter and more compressed. When its temperature reaches 18 million°F (10 million°C), it becomes a new star.

The center becomes a hot, dense protostar (a very young star).

Matter spirals in.

In a whirl

When cores of matter collapse during star formations, they start to rotate and heat up. The collapsing matter forms a disc as a result of the rotation.

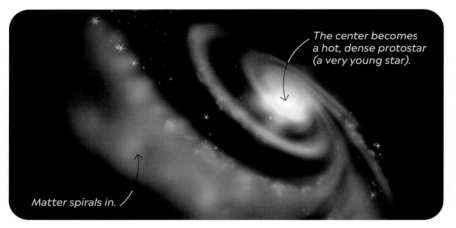

Matter is pulled in by gravity.

The disc heats up closer to the star.

Birth pangs

A newborn star is surrounded by a swirling disc of matter until powerful stellar winds force it away from the star's poles as twin jets.

The disc is more stable at a distance from the star.

Stellar winds blow material out in jets.

Stellar nurseries

Stars are being born in vast numbers in giant gas clouds everywhere, such as M16 (or the Eagle Nebula). Telescope pictures show dark columns nicknamed "the pillars of creation" (above), where star formation takes place. At the edges of the pillars, pockets of gas are collapsing to form stars.

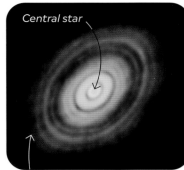

Central star

Dust disc shines at infrared and radio wavelengths.

Worlds beyond

Material that remains in orbit around a newborn star often comes together to form new planets. More than 5,300 exoplanets—planets orbiting stars other than our sun—have been found in recent decades. The ALMA radio telescope captured this image (left) of material around a newborn star separating into rings that may eventually form planets.

First discoveries

Astronomers detected the first exoplanets in 1992, orbiting a dead star called a pulsar. Three years later came the discovery of the first exoplanet orbiting close to a sunlike star, 51 Pegasi. This Jupiter-like world is now called Dimidium.

Artist's impression of the different types of exoplanets

Many exoplanets

Exoplanets can be very different from the planets of our solar system. They range from "hot Jupiters" (gas giants that orbit very close to their stars) and super-Earths (rocky planets far larger than our own), down to tiny worlds far smaller than Mercury. Some have temperatures hot enough to boil metal; others are covered in deep, planet-wide oceans; and some even produce cometlike tails of gas.

The **most massive** known **exoplanet** is HR 2562 b, with over **30 times the mass of Jupiter**.

LOOKING FOR EXOPLANETS

Exoplanets are much too faint to be seen directly. Astronomers try to find them indirectly, by observing the effect they have on their star. When viewed from Earth, the light from a distant star may appear to dim slightly, possibly due to an exoplanet coming in between the star and Earth during its orbit around its star. This tiny dip in the star's light is often taken as evidence for the existence of an exoplanet.

Star

An exoplanet passes in front of its star, temporarily lowering its brightness.

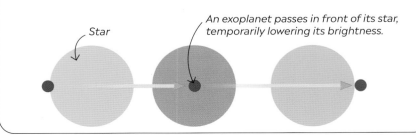

Star death

Stars burst into life by fusing hydrogen into helium in nuclear reactions in their cores. They shine until they use up their hydrogen fuel—then they start to die. First they brighten and swell into red giants and supergiants. Low-mass stars puff off their outer layers and fade away. High-mass stars die in a supernova explosion.

Live fast, die young

Stars bigger than the sun have hotter, denser cores. They burn their hydrogen fuel more quickly and live for only a few million years.

Core (not shown to scale) develops "onion layers."

Fates of stars

How long a star can keep burning hydrogen depends on its mass. Stars like the sun burn their fuel slowly and can shine for 10 billion years.

Red giant

When a star uses up the hydrogen in its core, fusion moves out to a shell around the center. The star's atmosphere then balloons outward. As the surface cools, the star becomes a red dwarf. As the core slowly collapses, it can trigger new nuclear reactions that extend the star's life by a few million years.

Supergiant

In massive stars, nuclear reactions continue inside the core, fusing atoms together to form heavier and heavier elements (including sodium, carbon, and oxygen), until iron is produced. The core gets so hot that the star balloons out to become a supergiant—a monster star many times larger than a normal red giant.

Planetary nebula

When the helium in a red giant's core runs out, it blows the star's layers into space. The escaping gas creates a planetary nebula, often with a complex shape—as seen in the Southern Ring Nebula, captured by the James Webb Space Telescope.

Supernova

Iron builds up rapidly in a supergiant's core. When this happens, the core can no longer generate enough outward pressure to balance the crushing force of gravity, and the star suddenly collapses. So much energy is released that the star blasts itself apart in a supernova explosion that can outshine a galaxy. The explosion scatters heavy elements across space, providing material for new stars.

Black hole

Neutron star

End states

The compressed remnant of the core often survives a supernova explosion, becoming either a superdense neutron star or—if the mass is high enough—a black hole.

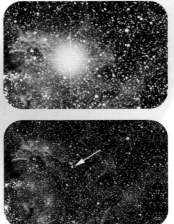

Modern find

In 1987, astronomers spotted a supernova (left) in the Large Magellanic Cloud, a close galaxy. The star that exploded was a blue giant called Sanduleak -69 202 (far left).

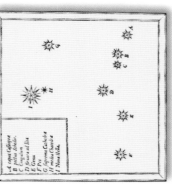

Star map made by Tycho Brahe

Spotting a supernova

Danish astronomer Tycho Brahe saw a supernova in 1572, which caused him to realize that the heavens were constantly changing.

White dwarf

Within a planetary nebula, the star's core continues to collapse until the electrons in its atoms are forced up against the central nuclei. This incredibly dense, hot star is called a white dwarf.

White dwarf pulls material off companion star.

Gas builds up on white dwarf's surface.

Gas ignites and burns off in a blast of fusion.

Companion star swells into red giant.

Companion is caught in blast.

Nova

A white dwarf in a binary system can attract enough gas from the other star to cause an explosion and make it into a nova, a new star.

51

The inner ring is one light-year across.

Jet from pulsar poles

Neutron star

Material blown out from the equator travels at half the speed of light.

Pulsar jet billows into clouds as it contacts interstellar gas.

Inside the crab

The pulsar in the Crab Nebula spins around 30 times a second, and pours out energy in the form of radio waves and X-rays.

At the **end**

When a star dies in a supernova, the force of the collapsing core is so great that atoms are broken down. The matter then gets compressed into a ball of neutrons and the core becomes a city-size neutron star, spinning as it emits pulses of radiation. When we detect pulses from a neutron star, we call it a pulsar. Larger collapsing cores crush the neutrons and make a dense core that light cannot escape from—a black hole. The enormous gravity of a black hole pulls in any nearby matter, letting nothing escape.

The crab pulsar

In 1054, Chinese astronomers saw a supernova explosion, which created the famous Crab Nebula. Buried inside the nebula is the collapsed core, which we detect as a pulsar.

Neutron stars

Neutron stars are tiny bodies that spin around rapidly. They are highly magnetic, so their magnetic field sweeps around rapidly as well. This generates radio waves, which are emitted as beams that we can see as pulsing signals. A neutron star is typically only 12 miles (20 km) across. Yet it can contain more than twice the sun's mass, making it incredibly dense.

Pulsar's rotation axis

Magnetic field

Neutron star

Jets from magnetic poles

Magnetic pole

Relatively shallow well

White dwarf

The gravitational pull of the object distorts space, causing other objects to "roll" toward it.

Steeper gravitational well

Neutron star

Paths of light rays passing close to black hole are bent.

Light that strays too close is sucked in.

Black hole forms a bottomless gravitational well.

Black holes

When a collapsing star's core is massive enough, it keeps shrinking as its gravity grows stronger. A black hole is a bottomless gravitational well, from which even light cannot escape.

Dark discs

We can't see a black hole, but we can detect one indirectly if it is part of a binary star system. Then, the matter it attracts from the other star forms a swirling disc around it, known as an accretion disc.

In 2016, astronomers discovered **two neutron stars** merging together to form a **new black hole**.

Black hole's binary companion

Hot spot where material from star contacts disc.

Superheated matter gives off X-rays as it falls into the black hole.

Gas close to center of disc is heated to 180 million°F (100 million°C).

Black hole at the center of the disc

Accretion disc surrounding black hole

The Milky Way

On a clear night, a hazy band of light arches across the sky, running through many of the best-known constellations. We call it the Milky Way. What we are seeing is a kind of "slice" through the collection of stars, or galaxy, to which the sun and all the other stars in the sky belong. It passes through the Cygnus, Perseus, and Cassiopeia constellations in the northern hemisphere, and the Centaurus, Crux, and Sagittarius constellations in the southern hemisphere.

Gas in the galactic center forms a "mini spiral."

Bar extends from either side of the central bulge.

The sun (located here) takes about 230 million years to circle the galactic center.

Our solar system is located about 26,000 light-years from the center of the Milky Way.

Milky Way myths

In the mythology of the Aztecs, the Milky Way was identified with Mixcoatl, the cloud-serpent god. In ancient Egypt and India, it was seen as the celestial mirror of rivers such as the Nile and Ganges.

Band across the sky

The Milky Way galaxy is a spiral, but from Earth it looks like a band stretching across the night sky. This is because we are seeing it from our position inside the galaxy's disc. Its brightest areas are most visible between June and September. Its dark patches are not starless regions, but areas in which dense dust clouds block the light from the stars behind them.

Milky Way star clouds in Scorpius and Sagittarius

Anatomy of the galaxy

Our galaxy is a vast system of around 200 billion stars. It is more than 100,000 light-years across but is mostly only about 1,000 light-years thick. The spiral arms emerging from its central bar form the disc of the galaxy. There are four main spiral arms, but two of these are more densely packed with stars than the others.

Side view of the Milky Way

This artist's impression of the Milky Way shows what our galaxy might look like viewed side-on from space. At the center is a glowing bulge, about 18,000 light-years in diameter, where stars are packed most densely. It also shows that the galaxy's bright "thin disc" of young stars, gas, and dust is embedded in a broader but dimmer and sparsely populated "thick disc" of older stars.

The Scutum-Centaurus arm blocks our view of the galactic center.

Sparse star clouds trail into the galactic halo region.

In a spin

The Milky Way galaxy spins around in space. We can tell this by looking at nearby galaxy Andromeda. The stars on one of its sides show a shift in spectral lines toward the blue, indicating they are moving toward us. The stars on the other side show a redshift, showing they are moving away.

Blueshift on the edge moving toward us.

Redshift on the edge moving away from us.

Red and blue shifts in the Andromeda galaxy

Supermassive monster

In 2022, astronomers used the Event Horizon Telescope (a series of globally linked radio telescopes) to create the first image of radiation from Sagittarius A*. Despite its enormous mass, the black hole at the center of this glowing ring is smaller than Mercury's orbit around the sun.

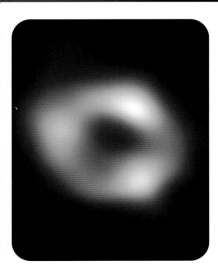

The galactic center

At the heart of our galaxy lies Sagittarius A*, a black hole with the mass of about four million suns. This Chandra X-ray Observatory image shows the gas clouds and central cluster of three million stars that surround Sagittarius A*, forming the galaxy's central bulge.

Massive stars close to central black hole

Glowing gas heated to 18 million°F (10 million°C)

Galactic neighbors

In far southern skies, two misty patches can be seen in the constellations Tucana and Dorado. They are nearby galaxies called the Large and Small Magellanic Clouds. The Large Magellanic Cloud lies just 160,000 light-years away from us and is irregular in shape, as is the Small Magellanic Cloud. Both of them, as well as our Milky Way, belong to a larger group of galactic neighbors called the Local Group.

Large Magellanic Cloud

Small Magellanic Cloud

Satellite galaxies

The Large Magellanic Cloud is 30,000 light-years across, less than one-third the size of the Milky Way. It contains much the same mix of stars and gas as our own galaxy. The Small Magellanic Cloud is only a quarter as big as the Large Cloud and lies slightly farther away. These galaxies were named after Portuguese navigator Ferdinand Magellan.

Baby galaxies

There are small galaxies closer to us than the Large Magellanic Cloud. The Sagittarius Dwarf Elliptical lies 80,000 light-years away, hidden behind the gas clouds in the center of our galaxy.

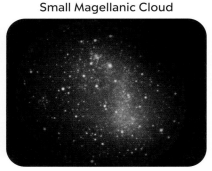

Milky Way

Sagittarius Dwarf Elliptical

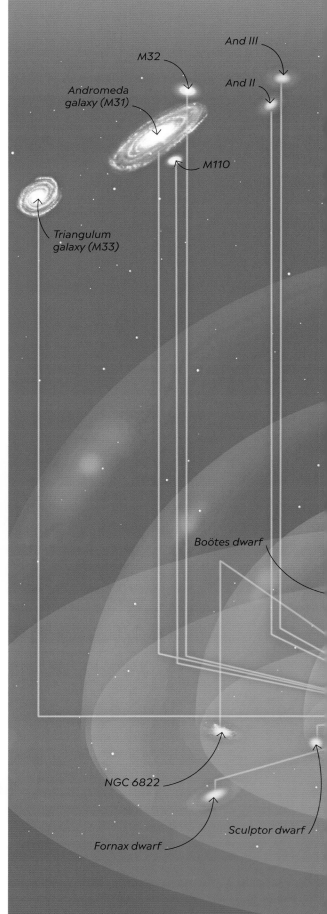

And III

M32

And II

Andromeda galaxy (M31)

M110

Triangulum galaxy (M33)

Boötes dwarf

NGC 6822

Sculptor dwarf

Fornax dwarf

The Local Group

The Milky Way is part of a larger collection of galaxies called the Local Group, which includes two more spiral galaxies in the constellations Andromeda and Triangulum. While this illustration shows only the major neighboring galaxies, there are at least 80 galaxies in the Local Group in total, held together by the power of gravity.

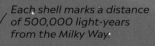
Each shell marks a distance of 500,000 light-years from the Milky Way.

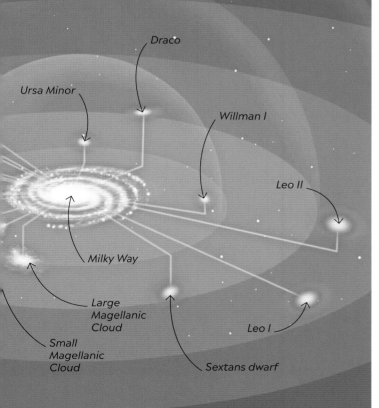

Draco

Ursa Minor

Willman I

Leo II

Milky Way

Large Magellanic Cloud

Leo I

Small Magellanic Cloud

Sextans dwarf

Dwarf elliptical galaxy M32

Andromeda, or M31 galaxy

Dwarf elliptical galaxy NGC 205

Giant neighbor

The Andromeda galaxy, also known as M31, is the largest spiral in the Local Group, with a diameter of about 150,000 light-years, but it probably has a similar mass to the Milky Way. Lying almost edge-on to our galaxy, it covers an area of sky bigger than two full moons, and its bright nucleus is easy to spot with binoculars.

Andromeda

The Andromeda galaxy looks like a fuzzy, moderately bright star in the northern skies. It lies close to the star Nu Andromedae in the Andromeda constellation.

Andromeda galaxy
Nu Andromedae

Star chart of the Andromeda constellation

The Triangulum galaxy

The bright galaxy M33 is the third spiral in the Local Group, after the Milky Way and Andromeda. M33 lies in the Triangulum constellation, close to the Andromeda galaxy. M33 is only just beyond naked-eye visibility—binoculars can spot it easily. The galaxy appears face-on to us, looking like a giant pinwheel.

Collisions between gas clouds create pressure waves that trigger the formation of new stars.

Newborn stars give off energy into the surrounding gas, creating glowing nebulae.

Galaxies **galore**

The Milky Way and the galaxies in the Local Group occupy only a tiny region of space. Scattered throughout the rest of space, across tens of billions of light-years, are at least 125 billion other galaxies. Many galaxies, including the Milky Way, are spiral in shape, while others are elliptical (oval) or lenticular (lens-shaped) or have no regular shape at all. Some galaxies are dwarfs, with fewer than a million stars, but others are giants with hundreds of billions of them.

Starburst region – a vast stellar nursery

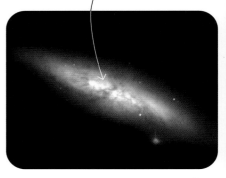

Irregular galaxies

Galaxies with no particular shape are classed as irregulars, such as M82 (above) in Ursa Major. Irregular galaxies are rich in gas and dust, and have many young stars.

GALAXY SHAPES

Edwin Hubble devised the method to classify galaxies as ellipticals (E), spirals (S), and barred spirals (SB), according to their shape.

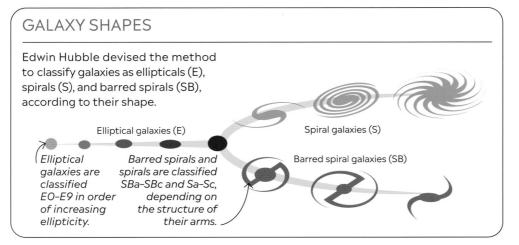

Elliptical galaxies (E)

Elliptical galaxies are classified E0–E9 in order of increasing ellipticity.

Barred spirals and spirals are classified SBa–SBc and Sa–Sc, depending on the structure of their arms.

Spiral galaxies (S)

Barred spiral galaxies (SB)

The largest known spiral galaxy, NGC 6872 is **five times wider** than the Milky Way.

Colliding galaxies

Typically, adjacent galaxies are 10 galaxy diameters apart. But sometimes two adjacent galaxies may drift closer together and collide. The vast gas clouds inside the galaxies crash into one another, triggering furious bouts of star formation, known as starbursts. As the stars in a galaxy are so far apart, two galaxies can collide without any of their stars crashing into each other.

Galactic nuclei remain intact the longest, held together by the gravity of central black holes.

Disrupted spiral arms lose their shape and unwind into space.

Colliding spiral galaxies
IC 2163 and NGC 2207

Galaxy cluster
Abell 2218

Clusters and superclusters

All galaxies interact with one another. Gravity binds them together into small groups and big clusters, which make up larger superclusters. Strings of superclusters form the structure of the universe.

Lenticular galaxies

Lens-shaped galaxies called lenticular galaxies are a cross between spiral and elliptical galaxies. They are spirals without the spiral arms and contain a central bulge of old stars.

Lenticular galaxy
NGC 6861

Elliptical galaxies

Elliptical galaxies include the smallest and largest galaxies. The biggest can be a million light-years across. Giant ellipticals such as M87 (left) are found in the heart of galaxy clusters.

Elliptical galaxies contain old yellow stars.

👁 EYEWITNESS

Edwin Hubble

US astronomer Edwin Hubble (1889–1953) transformed our view of the scale and history of the universe. In 1925, he proved that some nebulae in the sky were independent galaxies. In 1929, his research revealed that most galaxies are moving away from us in space due to cosmic expansion (see p.14). NASA's Hubble Space Telescope (see pp.16–17) was named after him.

Radio galaxies

NGC 5128 is an elliptical radio galaxy and the nearest active galaxy to us, at just 15 million light-years away. This picture enhances the visible light view of the central region with additional views—an X-ray view is colored blue and a radio wave view is colored red and orange. As can be seen, this galaxy is giving off huge amounts of radio waves.

Active galaxies

Most galaxies shine with the energy of hundreds of billions of stars, but active galaxies give out much more. These highly energetic galaxies include Seyfert galaxies with unusually bright centers, radio galaxies surrounded by vast clouds of radio-emitting gas, and quasars and blazars—objects that are the bright cores of galaxies billions of light-years away, generating vast amounts of light and other radiation from a tiny central region.

Looking at quasars

In 1960, US astronomer Allan Sandage helped discover quasars ("quasi-stellar radio sources") when he identified radio source 3C48 (an object in space that was emitting radio waves) as a starlike object. Later scientists identified it as a quasar with a large redshift.

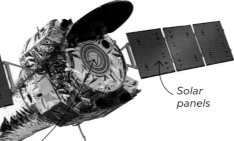

Solar panels

Camera

Polished metal mirror assembly used to reflect and focus X-rays

Radiation sources

Violent activity in active galaxies produces high-energy radiation such as gamma rays and X-rays. The Chandra X-ray Observatory (left) studies X-rays from sources in space.

Faint spiral arms 36,000 light-years across

Ring of intense starbirth around core

Bright core powered by black hole.

Quasars and blazars

Quasars (left) are the brightest objects in the universe. They are active galaxies billions of light-years away from Earth. When a jet from an active galaxy's center points toward Earth, we see a blazar.

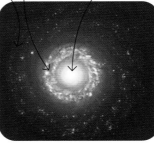

Seyfert galaxy NGC 7742

Seyfert galaxies

Some spiral galaxies have particularly bright centers and are classed as Seyfert galaxies. They are now thought to be closer and less powerful versions of quasars. About one in ten large spiral galaxies appear to be Seyferts.

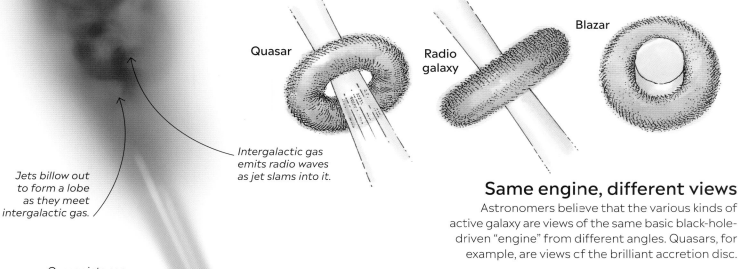

Quasar

Radio galaxy

Blazar

Intergalactic gas emits radio waves as jet slams into it.

Same engine, different views

Astronomers believe that the various kinds of active galaxy are views of the same basic black-hole-driven "engine" from different angles. Quasars, for example, are views of the brilliant accretion disc.

Jets billow out to form a lobe as they meet intergalactic gas.

Quasar jets can travel at almost the speed of light.

Material in disc is heated up by friction and gravity, emitting brilliant light and X-rays.

Dense ring of gas and dust surrounds central engine.

Collapsing gas clouds make supermassive black holes.

Stars straying too close to the black hole are torn to pieces.

The mass of the central black hole is millions or billions of times that of the sun.

Accretion disc is fueled by gas clouds and stars.

Galaxy engines

An active galaxy's central "engine" is a supermassive black hole. It is surrounded by a disc of stars as well as gas and dust that are spiraling in toward the center, drawn in by the black hole's immense gravitational pull. This disc emits radiation and subatomic particles as it heats up.

Black hole's intense magnetic field drives jets of particles and radiation out from poles.

Flattened accretion disc of material spiraling onto black hole.

Radio lobes are much farther away in reality.

A universe of life

We know of no other place where life exists. But with billions of sunlike stars in our galaxy alone, some of them are likely to have planets capable of supporting life. Scientists are looking for signs of life in our own solar system and beyond, using telescopes and space probes.

Crab on a volcanic vent

Europa

If life exists elsewhere in our solar system, then one of the most likely places to find it would be on Jupiter's moon Europa. Europa's icy crust conceals a global salty ocean with more water than all of Earth's water bodies put together. In late 2024, NASA plans to launch its Clipper spacecraft, which will fly by Europa to study it up close.

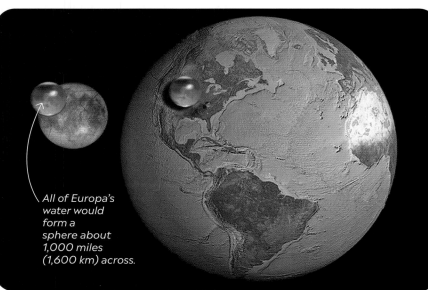

All of Europa's water would form a sphere about 1,000 miles (1,600 km) across.

Europa (left) is much smaller than Earth (right) but may contain more water.

Extreme environments

Scientists now know that life can thrive in hostile environments, such as in the superheated water around volcanic vents on the ocean floor. The discovery of life in such extreme environments on Earth suggests that life could exist in similarly hostile environments beyond Earth.

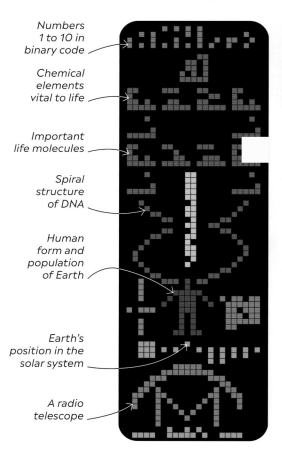

Numbers 1 to 10 in binary code

Chemical elements vital to life

Important life molecules

Spiral structure of DNA

Human form and population of Earth

Earth's position in the solar system

A radio telescope

Harbingers of life

All life on Earth is based on carbon-containing chemicals called organic molecules. Organic molecules have been found in the gas clouds that exist between the stars. This suggests that life might exist elsewhere in the universe. Some scientists even think that a comet or asteroid may have brought these building blocks of life to Earth.

Talking to aliens

The first message humankind transmitted to aliens was sent in 1974 as a set of 1,679 on-off digital pulses. With black squares for 1s and white squares for 0s, a pattern or pictogram is produced that forms a message. This was one of the earliest attempts at making contact with alien life. It eventually led to the formation of the SETI (Search for Extraterrestrial Intelligence) Institute in 1984.

Goldilocks zone

If a planet is too close to its star, it will be too hot to support life. If it is too far away, it will be too cold. The "Goldilocks zone" is the habitable zone around a star where the temperature is just right for liquid water to exist, and therefore to support life. In 2015, NASA's Kepler Space Telescope discovered an Earth-size exoplanet (see p.49) called Kepler-186f in the habitable zone of the red dwarf star Kepler-186. Of all the exoplanets discovered so far, hundreds of them lie in the habitable zones of their stars.

Artist's impression of Kepler-186f

Arecibo calling

The message for alien life (see facing page) was beamed at a cluster of 300,000 stars from the Arecibo radio telescope in 1974. It will reach them in 25,000 years.

The Sounds of Earth record, carried aboard the Voyager probes

Records of Earth

In the early 1970s, the Pioneer 10 and 11 space probes traveling out of the solar system carried small metal plaques that identified their time and place of origin for any aliens that might find them in the future.

To paint a picture of our world for alien civilizations, the Voyager 1 and 2 space probes, which were launched in the late 1970s, carried gold-plated discs with sounds and images of life on Earth.

 EYEWITNESS

Ramiro Saide

Young Mozambican scientist Ramiro Saide, an intern at the US SETI Institute, has studied what possible alien civilizations living in nearby star systems might find when they look toward Earth. Our planet's mobile towers and radio stations produce a lot of "radio noise," which may be picked up by aliens. However, Saide believes that an alien civilization would need to be more advanced than ours to detect these signals from a distance.

Star maps

Earth's sky is divided into 88 constellations, or star patterns. These two maps will help you identify the constellations. The first shows stars visible from Earth's northern hemisphere, and the second from the southern hemisphere. Over the course of the year, as Earth orbits the sun, different stars become visible.

Northern hemisphere stars

One point in the sky never moves. This fixed point is known as the celestial pole. In the northern hemisphere, Polaris is almost exactly on the celestial north pole. It is the brightest star in the Ursa Minor constellation. To use the chart on the right, turn the book so the current month is at the bottom. Northern hemisphere observers should then face south to see the stars in the map's lower part.

This view of Taurus shows the star Aldebaran at the lower left, below the Hyades star cluster.

RECOGNIZING CONSTELLATIONS

The Big Dipper

Some stars within constellations are easy to spot, such as the seven stars in the back of Ursa Major, the Great Bear. They are known as the Big Dipper.

Position of the Big Dipper in Ursa Major

The red lines work like latitude and longitude on Earth.

The Double Cluster is two dense groupings of stars (left and right of center).

JUNE · JULY · AUGUST · SEPTEMBER · OCTOBER · NOVEMBER · DECEMBER · JANUARY · FEBRUARY · MARCH · APRIL · MAY

NORMA · ARA · SCORPIUS · TELESCOPIUM · CORONA AUSTRALIS · SAGITTARIUS · SERPENS CAUDA · SCUTUM · INDUS · GRUS · SCULPTOR · PHOENIX · FORNAX · ERIDANUS · CÆLUM · COLUMBA · CARINA · PUPPIS · LEPUS · ORION · MONOCEROS · CANIS MAJOR · PYXIS · VELA · ANTLIA · HYDRA · SEXTANS · CRATER · CORVUS · CENTAURUS · HYDRA · VIRGO · LIBRA · LUPUS · OPHIUCHUS · SERPENS CAPUT · BOÖTES · CORONA BOREALIS · COMA BERENICES · LEO · LEO MINOR · CANCER · GEMINI · CANIS MINOR · AURIGA · TAURUS · CAMELOPARDALIS · LYNX · URSA MAJOR · CANES VENATICI · DRACO · URSA MINOR · Polaris · CEPHEUS · CASSIOPEIA · Double Cluster · PERSEUS · ANDROMEDA · TRIANGULUM · ARIES · PISCES · CETUS · PEGASUS · AQUARIUS · DELPHINUS · VULPECULA · SAGITTA · AQUILA · EQUULEUS · HERCULES · LYRA · CYGNUS · PISCIS AUSTRINUS · MICROSCOPIUM · CAPRICORNUS · Aldebaran · Pleiades

Key to the map

☀ Star clusters   — Constellations
· Stars   ···· Path of the sun

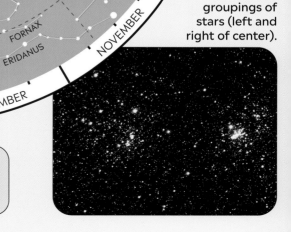

The Milky Way is broadest and brightest in the constellations of Sagittarius and Scorpius. In this region of the sky, we are looking toward the very center of our galaxy.

The Carina Nebula, in the constellation of Carina, is brightly illuminated by stars embedded within its gas and dust.

Southern stars

Unlike the northern hemisphere sky, the southern hemisphere sky does not have a pole star. The celestial south pole is just a blank area of sky. To use the chart on the right, turn the book so the current month is at the bottom. Observers in the southern hemisphere will see the stars in the lower part of the map in their northern skies.

The Fornax Cluster is mostly made up of elliptical galaxies.

The light-blue areas represent the Milky Way— the stars of our galaxy's disc.

JULY
JUNE
AUGUST
MAY
SEPTEMBER
APRIL
OCTOBER
MARCH
NOVEMBER
FEBRUARY
DECEMBER
JANUARY

DRACO
HERCULES
CORONA BOREALIS
LYRA
CYGNUS
SAGITTA
OPHIUCHUS
SERPENS CAPUT
BOOTES
AQUILA
SERPENS CAUDA
LIBRA
CANES VENATICI
SCUTUM
Heart of the Milky Way
SCORPIUS
VIRGO
DELPHINUS
CAPRICORNUS
SAGITTARIUS
CORONA AUSTRALIS
LUPUS
COMA BERENICES
CEPHEUS
EQUULEUS
PISCES AUSTRINUS
NORMA
ARA TELESCOPIUM
CENTAURUS
CORVUS
CRATER
LEO
AQUARIUS
GRUS
INDUS
PAVO
TRIANGULUM AUSTRALE
CRUX
SEXTANS
URSA MAJOR
LACERTA
PEGASUS
MICROSCOPIUM
TUCANA
OCTANS
APUS CHAMAELEON
CIRCINUS
MUSCA
CARINA
Carina Nebula
ANTLIA
LEO MINOR
PISCES
SCULPTOR
PHOENIX
HYDRUS
MENSA
DORADO VOLANS
RETICULUM
VELA
PYXIS
HYDRA
CANCER
MARCH
CASSIOPEIA
CETUS
HOROLOGIUM
PICTOR
PUPPIS
CANIS MAJOR
ANDROMEDA
FORNAX
Fornax Cluster
COLUMBA
LEPUS
Sirius
MONOCEROS
CANIS MINOR
GEMINI
ARIES
ERIDANUS
ORION
LYNX
TAURUS
PERSEUS
AURIGA

Key to the map

* ★ Star clusters
* ● Stars
* ── Constellations
* ⋯ Path of the sun

The Fornax Cluster is mostly made up of elliptical galaxies.

Sirius (center) is the brightest star in the entire sky. For southern-hemisphere stargazers, the constellation Orion lies to its left.

Discovery timeline

Humans have studied the universe for at least 5,000 years. Recently, we have pieced together the universe's story, from its beginning in the Big Bang around 13.8 billion years ago to the present day.

Saturn's rings, described correctly in 1655

The Crab Nebula, the remnant of a supernova seen in 1054

c. 4000 BCE The Egyptians, Chaldeans, and Hindus name bright stars and identify patterns of stars as constellations.

c. 2000 BCE Lunar and solar calendars are introduced.

550 BCE Pythagoras, a Greek mathematician, suggests that the sun, moon, Earth, and planets are spherical.

360 BCE Aristotle, a Greek philosopher, proposes that the planets are stuck in rotating crystal spheres and that all stars are the same distance away. He states that the universe is made from a combination of fire, water, earth, and air.

290 BCE In Greece, the astronomer Aristarchus uses lunar eclipse timings to show that the distance between Earth and the moon is equal to about 31 times Earth's width, and that the moon is just over one-quarter the size of Earth.

150 BCE Greek astronomer Hipparchus measures the length of the year to an accuracy of six minutes. He catalogs the position and brightness of stars and states that the sun's orbit around Earth is elliptical.

c. 130 CE Greek mathematician Ptolemy writes *The Almagest*, which summarizes the astronomical knowledge of the time.

c. 800 Arab astronomers refine astronomical knowledge, including defining the ecliptic and the orbital periods of the sun, moon, and planets.

1054 Chinese astronomers record a supernova in the constellation of Taurus.

1252 In Spain, King Alphonso X commissions the Alphonsine Tables, which list planetary positions.

1420 The Mongol ruler Ulugh Beg builds an observatory in Samarkand (in present-day Uzbekistan). His catalog of naked-eye star positions is the first since that of Hipparchus.

1543 Nicolaus Copernicus, a Polish astronomer, publishes *On the Revolutions of the Heavenly Spheres*. It signals the end of the idea of an Earth-centered universe.

1572 Danish nobleman Tycho Brahe observes a supernova in Cassiopeia and shows that it lies beyond the moon. Stars are thus not a fixed distance away.

1596 Tycho Brahe finishes 20 years of highly accurate planetary observations.

1609 German astronomer Johannes Kepler devises two laws. First, that planets have elliptical orbits, with the sun at one focus of the ellipse. Second, that a planet moves fastest when close to the sun.

1610 In Italy, Galileo Galilei publishes the results of his telescopic studies in *Sidereus Nuncius*. These show that the moon is mountainous, Jupiter has four moons, and the sun is spotty and rotates.

Galileo states that the phases of Venus indicate that the sun, not Earth, lies at the solar system's center.

1619 Johannes Kepler devises his third law, which describes the mathematical relationship between a planet's orbital period and its distance from the sun.

1655 Christiaan Huygens, a Dutch mathematician and astronomer, correctly describes Saturn's ring system and discovers Saturn's moon, Titan.

1675 In Denmark, Ole Rømer uses the eclipse times of Jupiter's moons to measure the speed of light.

1686 English astronomer Edmond Halley shows that "his" comet is periodic and part of the solar system. It sweeps past the sun every 76 years.

1687 Isaac Newton, an English physicist, publishes his theory of gravity in *Principia*. It explains why the planets orbit the sun.

1761 and 1769 Astronomers observe the transits of Venus across the face of the sun, which are used to calculate the distance between the sun and Earth.

Edmond Halley was the first to calculate the orbit of a comet, which was later named after him.

1769 The first predicted return of a comet (Halley's) proves that the laws of gravity extend at least to the edge of the solar system.

1781 German British astronomer William Herschel discovers the planet Uranus.

1784 A list of 103 "fuzzy" nebulae is drawn up by Frenchman Charles Messier.

1785 William Herschel describes the shape of the Milky Way galaxy.

1801 Giuseppe Piazzi, an Italian monk, discovers Ceres, the first asteroid.

1815 Joseph von Fraunhofer maps the dark lines in the solar spectrum.

1838 German astronomer Friedrich Bessel calculates that the star 61 Cygni is 11 light-years away.

1840 In the US, the moon is photographed by scientist John W. Draper. It is the first photo to record astronomical data.

1846 Neptune is discovered by using Newton's laws of gravitation.

1864 In England, William Huggins uses a spectrometer to show that comets contain carbon and that stars consist of the same chemical elements as Earth.

1890 About 30 stellar distances (distances of stars from Earth) have now been measured.

1900 New knowledge of the radioactive decay of elements leads to the realization that Earth is more than 1 billion years old.

1905 Albert Einstein proposes that $E = mc^2$, meaning that energy (E) can be produced by destroying mass (m). This is the breakthrough in understanding energy generation in stars.

1910 By plotting stellar temperature and luminosity, astronomers Ejnar Hertzsprung and Henry Russell find that there are only two main groups of stars—"dwarfs" and "giants."

1912 US astronomer Henrietta Leavitt finds that the time periods between the maximum brightnesses of giant variable stars called Cepheid stars are related to their luminosities.

1917 The 8.2 ft (2.5 m) Hooker Telescope on Mount Wilson, California, is used for the first time.

Charged-coupled device (CCD), 1980

1920 US scientist Harlow Shapley finds that the sun is two-thirds of the way toward the edge of the Milky Way.

1925 Cecilia Payne-Gaposchkin, an Anglo-American astronomer, shows that 75 percent of a star's mass is hydrogen.

1926 British astronomer Arthur Eddington finds that for most of a star's life, its luminosity is dependent on its mass.

1927 US astronomer Edwin Hubble shows that the universe is expanding.

Cecilia Payne-Gaposchkin, 1925

1930 Pluto is discovered by US astronomer Clyde Tombaugh.

1931 US physicist Karl Jansky detects radio waves from the Milky Way's center.

1931 Astronomer Georges Lemaître suggests that all matter in the universe started as a single, highly condensed sphere. This exploded in a "Big Bang."

1939 Physicist Hans Bethe shows how destroying hydrogen and producing helium yields stellar energy.

1955 Scientists Fred Hoyle and Martin Schwarzschild show how helium changes into carbon and oxygen in giant stars and how higher elements like cobalt and iron are made before massive stars explode.

1963 The first quasar, 3C48, is identified.

1965 Astronomers Arno Penzias and Robert Wilson discover cosmic microwave background radiation (CMBR).

1967 Belfast-born Jocelyn Bell Burnell discovers the first pulsar.

1971 The first black hole Cygnus X-1 is discovered due to its effect on its companion star.

1980 In the US, astronomer Vera Rubin finds that many galaxies contain dark matter that affects their spin speed.

1980 US cosmologist Alan Guth modifies the Big Bang theory. He introduces "inflation," whereby the very young universe expands from the size of a proton to the size of a watermelon in an instant.

1980 Charged-coupled devices (the electronic chips in digital cameras) are used in astronomy. They are nearly 100 percent efficient at converting light into electronic signals.

1992 The first Kuiper Belt object is discovered by astronomers David Jewitt and Jane Luu.

1992 Exoplanets—planets orbiting stars other than the sun—are discovered.

1995 The first exoplanet orbiting an ordinary main sequence star, 51 Pegasi, is discovered.

2006 The category of dwarf planets is introduced after the discovery of Eris. Pluto is reclassified as a dwarf planet.

2011 The Nobel Prize in Physics is awarded for the discovery of the accelerating expansion of the universe.

2015 Astronomers detect the first gravitational waves—ripples in space triggered by the collision of two black holes.

2019 The Event Horizon Telescope project produces the first-ever image of a black hole.

2022 The James Webb Space Telescope begins capturing light from the earliest galaxies in the universe.

Artist's impression of Eris

Find out **more**

Books are a great way to find out about the universe, but you may want to be more than an armchair astronomer. Start by looking up and exploring the sky for yourself, or join a society of other amateur astronomers. You can also visit planetariums, observatories, museums, and space centers.

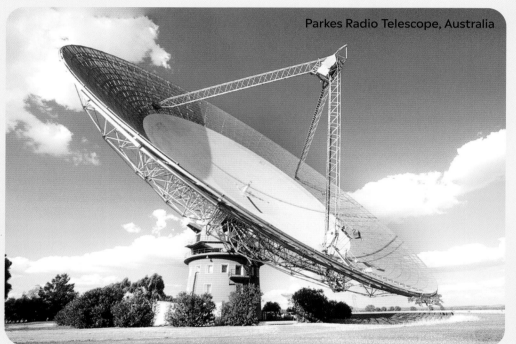
Parkes Radio Telescope, Australia

Tanegashima Space Center, Japan

Space centers
Some space centers have public viewing areas where you can watch the launch of a rocket or see space engineers preparing the next generation of spacecraft.

Radio telescopes
Unlike optical telescopes, radio telescopes are sited on low-lying ground and are more accessible. You can get up close to the telescopes and learn about them in the visitor centers.

Observatories
Today's world-class optical observatories are built on mountaintop locations far from inhabited areas. Those situated at lower altitudes have public access programs. You can look around the observatory site and a few observatories will even let you gaze through a telescope.

PLACES TO VISIT

Kennedy Space Center, Florida, US
This space complex sent people to the moon and launched NASA's Space Shuttles. Tour the exhibits and watch preparations for a future launch.

Mauna Kea Observatories, Hawai'i, US
The dormant volcano is home to 13 telescopes, including Keck I and Keck II, two of the largest telescopes in the world.

Noordwijk Space Expo, the Netherlands
The European Space Agency's visitor exhibition narrates the story of space exploration and has a planetarium showing simulations of space.

Yerkes Observatory, US

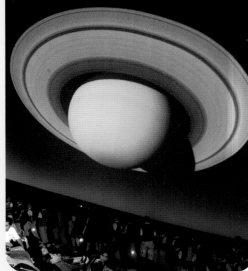

USEFUL WEBSITES

- The universe in a series of maps:
  www.atlasoftheuniverse.com/index.html

- Lunar phases, day length, and calendars:
  aa.usno.navy.mil/faq/index

- Japanese space facilities:
  global.jaxa.jp

- The Royal Observatory Greenwich,
  London, UK: **www.rmg.co.uk/
  royal-observatory**

- The Mars Express spacecraft:
  **www.esa.int/Science_Exploration/
  Space_Science/Mars_Express**

- European Southern Observatory, Chile:
  www.eso.org/public

- Mauna Kea Observatories, Hawai'i, US:
  www.ifa.hawaii.edu

- The Kennedy Space Center:
  www.kennedyspacecenter.com

- The latest from the Hubble Space
  Telescope: **hubblesite.org**

- Join the mission to find life beyond Earth
  with SETI institute: **www.seti.org**

- Details of NASA's space exploration:
  www.nasa.gov/missions/index.html

- The James Webb Space Telescope:
  webb.nasa.gov

- Past, present, and future eclipses:
  solarsystem.nasa.gov/eclipses/home

- Details of NASA's Mars exploration:
  mars.nasa.gov

- Asteroids that travel close to Earth:
  cneos.jpl.nasa.gov

- Planetary facts at your fingertips: **nssdc.
  gsfc.nasa.gov/planetary**

- Details of NASA's exoplanet exploration:
  exoplanets.nasa.gov

- Fun with NASA's Kids' Club:
  www.nasa.gov/kidsclub/index.html

- Imagining yourself as an astronaut with
  NASA: **www.jpl.nasa.gov/edu/learn/
  project/imagine-youre-
  an-astronaut**

Planetariums and museums

A visit to a planetarium—an indoor theater where images of space are projected above your head—will help you become familiar with the night sky. Get to know the constellations before being transported across space to see planets and stars up close.

Planetario Mutec, Mexico City

Home skywatching

On a clear, moonless night in the city, you will be able to pick out around 300 stars using your eyes alone, and 10 times more will be visible from a dark, rural location. Binoculars reveal even more stars. Telescopes bring the objects even closer, making them appear brighter and larger.

Viewing with binoculars

Tube houses mirror that collects and focuses starlight.

Light enters telescope

Finder telescope to locate object

Eyepiece

Mount supports telescope and automatically turns it to keep pace with the sky.

Portable telescope for home and countryside

Tripod stand

Joining a group or society

Skywatching with others is a great way to learn. National societies and associations publish journals and hold meetings. You can also find local amateur astronomical organizations in many towns and cities. Some of these have their own telescopes and hold regular observing sessions.

Glossary

ACTIVE GALAXY A galaxy emitting an exceptional amount of energy, much of which comes from a central supermassive black hole.

ASTEROID A small rocky body orbiting the sun. Most asteroids orbit in the Asteroid Belt between Mars and Jupiter.

ASTRONOMY The study of everything in space, including space itself.

ATMOSPHERE The layer of gas around a star or planet or another body in space, held in place by gravity.

AURORA The colorful light display of glowing gas in the upper atmosphere above a planet's polar regions.

BARRED SPIRAL GALAXY A galaxy with spiral arms that curl out from the ends of a bar-shaped nucleus.

BIG BANG The explosion that created the universe.

BINARY STAR A pair of stars, each of which revolves around the overall center of mass of the two-star system.

BLACK HOLE A compact region of space where the mass of a dense star has collapsed and whose gravity stops anything from escaping.

BLAZAR An active galaxy with a supermassive black hole at its center.

BRIGHTNESS A measure of the light of a star as seen from Earth (*see* Luminosity).

BROWN DWARF A star with too little mass to start the nuclear fusion process that powers a normal star.

CLUSTER A group of stars or galaxies that are gravitationally bound together.

COMET A small body of snow, ice, and dust orbiting the sun beyond the planets.

Comet McNaught, 2007

Barringer Crater, Arizona, US

CONSTELLATION One of the 88 areas of Earth's sky whose bright stars form a recognizable pattern.

CORONA The outermost region of the sun's atmosphere.

COSMOLOGY The study of the universe as a whole, and its origin and evolution.

CRATER A bowl-shaped hollow in the surface of a planet, dwarf planet, moon, asteroid, or comet.

DARK ENERGY A form of energy that makes up 68 percent of the universe.

DARK MATTER A substance that makes up 27 percent of the universe.

DOUBLE STAR Two stars that appear very close together in Earth's sky, but which in reality are physically separate.

DWARF PLANET A small, near-spherical body orbiting the sun.

ECLIPSE An effect due to the passage of one space body into the shadow of another. In a solar eclipse, the moon covers the sun. In a lunar eclipse, the moon moves into Earth's shadow.

ECLIPTIC The yearly path followed by the sun in Earth's sky.

ELECTROMAGNETIC RADIATION The energy waves given off by space objects. These include light, X-rays, and radio and infrared wavelengths.

ELLIPTICAL GALAXY A round- or elliptical-shaped galaxy.

EXTRASOLAR PLANET (EXOPLANET) A planet orbiting a star other than the sun.

EXTRATERRESTRIAL LIFE A life form not originating on Earth.

GALAXY A grouping of a vast number of stars, gas, and dust held together by gravity.

GAS GIANT A large planet that consists predominantly of hydrogen and helium, which are in gaseous form at the planet's visible surface.

GLOBULAR CLUSTER A near-spherical cluster of old stars found predominantly in the halo of a galaxy.

GRAVITY A force of attraction found throughout the universe.

HERTZSPRUNG-RUSSELL (H-R) DIAGRAM A diagram in which stars are plotted according to their luminosity and surface temperature, and which shows different classes of stars, such as giants and dwarfs.

Neptune, a gas giant

INTERSTELLAR MEDIUM Gas and dust between the stars in a galaxy.

IRREGULAR GALAXY A galaxy with no obvious shape or structure.

KUIPER BELT The belt of rock and ice bodies that orbit the sun beyond Neptune.

LENTICULAR GALAXY A galaxy in the shape of a convex lens.

LIGHT-YEAR A unit of distance. One light-year is the distance light travels in one year: 5.9 trillion miles (9.5 trillion km).

LOCAL GROUP The cluster of at least 80 galaxies that includes the Milky Way.

LUMINOSITY The total amount of energy emitted in one second by a star.

MAIN SEQUENCE STAR A star that shines steadily by converting hydrogen into helium.

MASS The amount of matter in an object.

METEOR A short-lived streak of light that is produced by a meteoroid as it travels through Earth's atmosphere.

METEORITE A piece of asteroid that has traveled through space and lands on a planet, dwarf planet, or moon.

METEOROID A piece of asteroid that burns up in the atmosphere of a planet, dwarf planet, or moon.

MILKY WAY The barred, spiral-shaped galaxy that includes the sun. Also the name of the path of stars in Earth's night sky that is our view of the galaxy's disc of stars.

MOON A body orbiting a planet, dwarf planet, or asteroid. Also called a natural satellite.

NEBULA A vast cloud of gas and dust in interstellar space (see Planetary nebula).

NEUTRON STAR An ultra-dense, compact star formed from the core of a star that explodes as a supernova.

NOVA A star that suddenly brightens at least a thousand-fold, and then fades back to normal brightness.

NUCLEAR FUSION The process that takes place within a star's core, whereby atomic nuclei join to form heavier atomic nuclei and energy is released.

NUCLEUS The body of a comet, the core of a galaxy, or the core of an atom.

OBSERVATORY A building housing telescopes.

OORT CLOUD A sphere of more than a trillion comets surrounding the planetary part of the solar system.

ORBIT The path taken by a body around another of greater mass.

Meteorite fragment

PHOTOSPHERE The gaseous but visible outer surface of the sun, or other star.

PLANET A massive round body that orbits a star.

PLANETARY NEBULA A late stage in the life of a star such as the sun.

PROTOSTAR An early stage in the formation of a star.

PULSAR A rapidly rotating neutron star identified by the brief pulses of energy we receive as it spins.

QUASAR An active galaxy that is exceptionally luminous.

RADIO GALAXY An active galaxy surrounded by clouds of radio-emitting gas.

RED GIANT A large, red, luminous star in its late stages.

SATELLITE A natural body orbiting another more massive body.

SEYFERT GALAXY An active spiral galaxy with a luminous and compact nucleus.

SHOOTING STAR An everyday name for a meteor.

SOLAR CYCLE An 11-year period of varying solar activity.

SOLAR SYSTEM The sun and all the bodies that orbit it.

SPACE The place beyond Earth's atmosphere; also the area between astronomical objects, such as planets, dwarf planets, stars, and galaxies.

SPECTRUM The colors produced by splitting light, for instance, from a star, into a rainbowlike spread.

SPEED OF LIGHT The constant speed at which light travels: 186,000 miles per second (299,792,458 km per second).

SPIRAL GALAXY A disc-shaped galaxy with spiral arms.

STAR A huge spinning sphere of very hot and very luminous gas.

SUNSPOT A dark, cool region on the visible surface of the sun or another star.

Spiral galaxy NGC 4414

SUPERCLUSTER A group of galaxy clusters.

SUPERGIANT A large, luminous star.

SUPERNOVA A massive star that has exploded and is up to a million times brighter than usual.

TELESCOPE An instrument that uses lenses or mirrors to collect and focus light to form an image of a distant object.

TERRESTRIAL PLANETS The solar system's four rocky planets: Mercury, Venus, Earth, and Mars.

UNIVERSE Everything that exists—all the galaxies, stars, and planets, and the space in between.

VARIABLE STAR A star whose brightness varies over time.

WHITE DWARF An end-stage in the life of a star.

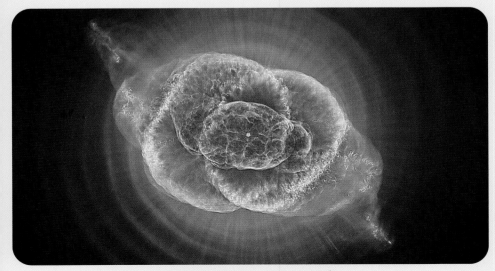

Cat's Eye Nebula (NGC 6543), a planetary nebula

Index

Acknowledgments

The publisher would like to thank the following people for their help with making the book: Peter Bull for his artworks, Jonathan Brooks and Sarah Mills for picture research, Carole Stott for assisting with the updates, Ben Hubbard and Chhavi Nagpal for editorial assistance, Prateek Maurya for design assistance, Hazel Beynon for proofreading, and Elizabeth Wise for the index.

The publisher would like to thank the following for their kind permission to reproduce their photographs:
(Key: a-above, b-below/bottom, c-center, f-far, l-left, r-right, t-top)

123RF.com: nasaimages 60t, Natalia Romanova 8-9c. **The 2df Galaxy Redshift Survey Team:** www.2dfgrs.net 9crb. **akg-images:** 39tr. **Alamy Images:** Danita Delimont / Russell Gordon 69tc. **Alamy Stock Photo:** Matteo Chinellato 38br, Mark Garlick 34cl, Dennis Hallinan 6-7c, IanDagnall Computing 7tr, 40bl, NASA / digitaleye / J Marshall - Tribaleye Images 39crb, NASA Archive 22cb, NG Images 41br, RGB Ventures / SuperStock / Roger Ressmeyer 40-41tc, RGB Ventures / SuperStock / Tony Hallas 7crb, Science History Images / Photo Researchers 34bc, 62cr, Science Photo Library / Mark Garlick 12tl, 31cra, Svintage Archive 39tc, UPI / NASA / JPL-Caltech / UMD 40c, Westend61 GmbH 57cra. **Anglo- Australian Observatory:** David Malin 51tr. **The Art Archive:** Musée du Louvre Paris / Dagli Orti (A) 27cr. **Bridgeman Art Library, London / New York:** Archives Charmet 46cl. **British Museum:** 6bl. **© CERN Geneva:** 2tr, 10br. **Corbis:** 62bc, Yann Arthus-Bertrand 8cl, Bettmann 3tl, 12bl, 32c, 59br, 67cl, Araldo de Luca 20cr, Charles & Josette Lenars 70tc, NASA 8clb, Robert Y. Ono 44br, Enzo & Paolo Ragazzini 6bc, Roger Ressmeyer 13tl, 63cl, 68br, 63bl, 69br, Paul A. Souders 29tl, Stapleton Collection 45bl. **DK Images:** Natural History Museum 71tc. **Dorling Kindersley:** Arran Lewis / NASA 28-29c, The Science Museum, London / Clive Streeter 4tr, 43bl. **Dreamstime. com:** Jeff Cleveland 16bl. **ESA:** C. Carreau / Schrder, Karkoschka et al (2012) 35crb, DLR / FU Berlin, NASA MGS MOLA Science Team 30crb, ESA and the Planck Collaboration - D. Ducros 13cra, ESA-C. Carreau / ATG medialab 41cr, Stefan Payne-Wardenaar / MPIA 55cra, NASA,

CSA, STScI, J. DePasquale, A. Koekemoer, A. Pagan (STScI). 48-49c. **European Space Agency:** 11crb, D. Ducros 17cra. **ESA / Hubble:** M. Kornmesser 38cb, NASA 42-43c, NASA / J. Barrington 59cr. **ESO:** 59bl, ALMA (NAOJ / NRAO) 49tc, EHT Collaboration 55bl. **© Stéphane Guisard:** 70bl. **Courtesy of JAXA:** 68tr. **Mary Evans Picture Library:** 8tl, 26bc, 27crb, 57tr. **Margaret Geller:** Scott Kenyon 8br. **Getty Images:** Bettmann 12bc, 59br, Corbis / Lawrence Manning 7cra, Corbis Historical 40clb, Sean Hunter: 29tc, Stone / Georgette Douwma 29br, Stone / Paul A. Souders 29tl, The Asahi Shimbun 45br. **Getty Images / iStock:** E+ / dszc 4clb, 17tr, E+ / nicolamargaret 4cra, 6c. **FLPA - Images of nature:** B. Borrell 22c, 22cl. **NASA:** 4crb, 9c, 9bl (x6), 16br, 18cl, 18cra, 19tr, 23crb, 23cr, 26-27, 27tr, 27br, 27bl, 29cra, 31cr, 33tr, 33bl, 35ac, 37cr, 38-39c, 55br, 58-59tc, Carnegie Mellon University 39cr, Clouds AO / SEarch 33th, ESA and The Hubble Heritage Team (STScI / AURA) 47bc, ESA, Amy Simon and the OPAL Team, and J. DePasquale (STScI) 11cla, ESA, and A. Simon (NASA Goddard) 2clb, 32-33c, ESA, H. Teplitz and M. Rafelski (IPAC / Caltech), ESA, HFI & LFI consortia (2010) 8bl, Goddard / Arizona State University 23cra, GSFC / Arizona State University 22-23c, GSFC / CIL / Adriana Manrique Gutierrez 5tr, 17b, JHUAPL / SwRI 37crb, HST Comet Science Team 32bc, JHUAPL 39tl, 39tc, JPL 8ca, 19br, 32c, 32bl, 33tc, 33cra, 33c, 33ac, 36clb, 36bc, 70cr, NASA HQ-GRIN 71cr, Johns Hopkins University Applied Physics Laboratory 21crb, Johns Hopkins University Applied Physics Laboratory / Southwest Research Institute 37cb, JPL 31cla, 34crb, JPL / DLR 62cl, JPL / Space Science Institute 35cra, JPL / University of Arizona / DLR 35bl, JPL / University of Arizona / University of Idaho 35bc, JPL-Caltech / ESA / CXC / Univ. of Ariz. / Univ. of Szeged 52crb, JPL-Caltech / MSSS 2b, 30-31tl, JPL-Caltech / R. Hurt (SSC / Caltech) 3cb, 54-55tc, JPL-Caltech / R. Hurt (SSC) 11br, JPL-Caltech / Space Science Institute 18cra, JPL-Caltech / UCLA / MPS / DLR / IDA 39bc, JPL-Caltech / Univ. of Arizona 31cb, NASA Ames / JPL-Caltech / T. Pyle 63t, SDO 2OI X-ray: Chandra (CXC), Optical: Hubble (STScI), Infrared: Spitzer (JPL-Caltech) 52t, X-ray: CXC / SAO / P. Plucinsky et al. 57br, A. Koekemoer (STScI), NOAO, ESA and The Hubble Heritage Team (STScI / AURA) 47tr, Courtesy of SOHO / Extreme Ultraviolet Imaging

Telescope (EIT) consortium 21cr, STScI 9tr, 49cra, 59cl, 60bl, 60br, 61crb, TRW 60cb, R. Windhorst (Arizona State University), and Z. Levay (STScI) 7bc. **Musée de la Poste, Paris:** 37cra. **National Maritime Museum:** NOAA: OAR / National Undersea Research Program (NURP) 62cra. **NOIRLab:** 14bl. **NOAO / AURA / NSF:** Pikaia: 2cra, 4cla, 9cl, 12bc, 14cr, 24-25, 27tc, 30l, 31clb, 36l, 37tl, 44bl, 48cl, 48bc, 52bc, 53b, 56bl, 61c, 62bl, 63br, 64br, 65tr. **Ramiro Saide:** 63bc. **Vicent Peris (OAUV / PTeam), astrophotographer of the Astronomical Observatory of the University of Valencia (OAUV):** MAST, STScI, AURA, NASA - Image processed with PixInsight at OAUV. Based on observations made with the NASA / ESA Hubble Space Telescope, obtained at the Space Telescope Science Institute, which is operated by the Association of Universities for Research in Astronomy, Inc., under NASA contract NAS 5-26555. 71bl. **Photolibrary:** Science Photo Library: 10tr, 38bc, Estate of Francis Bello 60cl, Lawrence Berkeley Laboratory 15cra, Dr Eli Brinks 55cr, Celestial Image Co. 47cr, 65bl, Bernhard Edmaier 28cl, Mark Garlick 19tl, 42-43t, 67br, Hale Observatories 52cr, David A Hardy 12-13, 36c, 51br, Harvard College Observatory 19cra, 43crb, Jerry Lodriguss 64bl, Allan Morton / Dennis Milon 54br, NASA 13tr, 28bl, 44cl, National Optical Astonomy Observatories 21crb, David Parker 67tc, Rev. Ronald Royer 21cl, John Sanford 42br, Jerry Schad 65tl, Dan Schechter 14tr, Eckhard Slawik 64tr, Babak A. Tafreshi: 65br. **Science Photo Library:** Richard Bizley 49cb, Mark Garlick 56-57c, Claus Lunau 41bl, I Macdonald / Oar / National Undersea Research Program / Texas A&M University / NOAA 62tr. **Shutterstock.com:** Pool / EPA-EFE / Marcio Jose Sanchez 53ca. **TopFoto:** Polfoto 28tr. **U.S. Geological Survey:** Howard Perlman, Hydrologist, USGS, Jack Cook, Woods Hole Oceanographic Institution, Adam Nieman, Igor Shiklamonov 62c.

All other images © Dorling Kindersley